SCHOLASTIC
LITERACY
PLACE

IT WORKS...AND KIDS LIKE IT!

SCHOLASTIC LITERACY PLACE

IT WORKS...AND KIDS LIKE IT!

Manageable Instructional Plans

Literacy Place follows a clear, consistent pattern of instruction and provides support for all learners. The Teacher's Edition includes explicit skills instruction and integrates the language arts.

The Strongest System for Beginning Readers

Literacy Place provides direct instruction in phonics and phonological awareness and fully reflects current and confirmed research.

Assessment Tools to Monitor and Modify Instruction

Literacy Place features focused assessment that informs

instruction and measures progress. The program offers

strategies targeting students who need skills intervention,

language-development support, and enrichment.

Power and Confidence for the Information Age

Literacy Place uses technology as an integral part

of learning while connecting the classroom to the

real world.

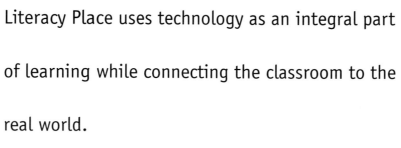

The Matrix

PERSONAL LITERACY	INTELLECTUAL LITERACY	SOCIAL LITERACY
Personal Voice	**Problem Solving**	**Teamwork**
We communicate in our unique voices as we grow and learn.	People have the power to solve problems.	Successful teams depend on the collaboration of individuals.

K

Stories About Us	See It, Solve It	All Together Now!
Big Idea We listen to, tell, and create stories.	**Big Idea** We see problems and find solutions.	**Big Idea** We share and help each other.
Mentor Grandmother: *Honey Wada*	**Mentor** Clay Animator: *Becky Wible*	**Mentor** Pizza Maker: *Kwaku Twumasi*
Place Storytelling Corner	**Place** Claymator's Studio	**Place** Restaurant
Project "All About Me" Class Book	**Project** Dramatization	**Project** Big Book of Menus

1

Hello!	Problem Patrol	Team Spirit
Big Idea We share what we like.	**Big Idea** There are many kinds of problems.	**Big Idea** It's fun to do things together.
Mentor Author: *Donald Crews*	**Mentor** Veterinarian: *Fay Vittetoe*	**Mentor** Soccer Coach: *Danny Prenat*
Place Writer's Home	**Place** Veterinarian's Office	**Place** Soccer Stadium
Project Scrapbook	**Project** Pet Care Guide	**Project** Game Rule Book

2

Snapshots	Super Solvers	Lights! Camera! Action!
Big Idea Our actions tell about us.	**Big Idea** There may be more than one way to solve a problem.	**Big Idea** Creative teams produce great performances.
Mentor Photographer: *Bruce Thorson*	**Mentor** Toy Designer: *Mary Rodas*	**Mentor** Theater Director: *Judith Martin*
Place Sports Arena	**Place** Toy Company	**Place** Children's Theater
Project Exhibit	**Project** Safety Poster Campaign	**Project** Play Production

3

What's New?	Big Plans	On the Job
Big Idea We learn about our world through new experiences.	**Big Idea** Making and using plans can help us solve problems.	**Big Idea** Teams work best when they use each member's strengths to get the job done.
Mentor Wilderness Guide: *Keith Jardine*	**Mentor** Architect: *Jack Catlin*	**Mentor** Art Director: *Max Jerome*
Place Wilderness School	**Place** Construction Site	**Place** Ad Agency
Project Anecdote	**Project** Floor Plan	**Project** Ad Campaign

4

Chapter by Chapter	What an Idea!	Discovery Teams
Big Idea We are always adding to our life story.	**Big Idea** People solve problems by inventing new things.	**Big Idea** When we work as a team, we learn new things about our world.
Mentor Author: *Jerry Spinelli*	**Mentor** Inventor: *Julie Lewis*	**Mentor** Astronaut: *Dr. Mae Jemison*
Place Bookstore	**Place** Inventor's Office	**Place** Space Center
Project Personal Narrative	**Project** Invention Marketing Plan	**Project** Multimedia Presentation

5

Making a Difference	It's a Mystery	Voyagers
Big Idea Each of us is inspired by the lives of others.	**Big Idea** We can solve mysteries using reason, logic, and intuition.	**Big Idea** We depend on a network of people when we explore.
Mentor Musician: *Joseph Shabalala*	**Mentor** Forensic Chemist: *Lilly Gallman*	**Mentor** Travel Agent: *Marie French*
Place Concert Hall	**Place** Detective Headquarters	**Place** Travel Agency
Project Tribute	**Project** Investigative Report	**Project** Travel Magazine

Look for the Unit-by-Unit Extensions in the Literacy Place area.

PERSONAL LITERACY
Creative Expression
People express themselves in many creative ways.

INTELLECTUAL LITERACY
Managing Information
Finding and using information helps us live in our world.

SOCIAL LITERACY
Community Involvement
Communities are built on the contributions of the people who live there.

Express Yourself
Big Idea We express ourselves through songs, sounds, stories, dance, and art.
Mentor Author: *Pat Mora*
Place Author's Studio
Project Storybook

I Spy!
Big Idea Information is all around us.
Mentor Farmer: *Steven Powell*
Place Gardening Center
Project Garden Journal

Join In!
Big Idea We help our community.
Mentor Singer/Songwriter: *Tom Chapin*
Place Performance Stage
Project Community Sing

Imagine That!
Big Idea Imagination lets us look at things in new ways.
Mentor Muralist: *William Walsh*
Place Artist's Studio
Project Story Mural

Information Finders
Big Idea Information comes from many sources.
Mentor Marine Biologist: *Laela Sayigh*
Place Aquarium
Project Big Book of Information

Home Towns
Big Idea We are all members of a community.
Mentor Mayor: *Steve Yamashiro*
Place Mayor's Office
Project Visitor's Map

Story Studio
Big Idea People express themselves through stories and pictures.
Mentor Author & Artist: *Tomie dePaola*
Place Author's Studio
Project Picture Book

Animal World
Big Idea We use information to understand the interdependence of people and animals.
Mentor Zoo Curator: *Lisa Stevens*
Place Zoo
Project Zoo Brochure

Lend a Hand
Big Idea People can make a difference in their communities.
Mentor Police Officer: *Nadine Jojola*
Place Police Station
Project Community Expo

Hit Series
Big Idea A creative idea can grow into a series.
Mentor Author & Illustrator: *Joanna Cole & Bruce Degen*
Place Publishing Company
Project New Episode

Time Detectives
Big Idea Finding information in stories and artifacts brings the past to life.
Mentor Archaeologist: *Dr. Ruben Mendoza*
Place Archaeological Site
Project Time Capsule

Community Quilt
Big Idea In a community, some things continue and some things change.
Mentor Community Garden Director: *Lorka Muñoz*
Place Community Garden
Project Community Quilt

The Funny Side
Big Idea Sometimes humor is the best way to communicate.
Mentor Cartoonist: *Robb Armstrong*
Place Cartoonist's Studio
Project Comic Strip

Nature Guides
Big Idea Gathering and using information help us understand and describe the natural world.
Mentor Park Ranger: *Veronica Gonzales-Vest*
Place National Park Headquarters
Project Field Guide

It Takes a Leader
Big Idea In every community there are people who inspire others to take action.
Mentor Editor: *Suki Cheong*
Place Newspaper Office
Project Op-Ed Page

In the Spotlight
Big Idea We use our creativity to reach an audience.
Mentor Drama Coach: *José García*
Place Actor's Workshop
Project Stage Presentation

America's Journal
Big Idea Considering different points of view gives us a fuller understanding of history.
Mentor Historian/Author: *Russell Freedman*
Place Historical Museum
Project Historical Account

Cityscapes
Big Idea Cities depend on the strengths and skills of the people who live and work there.
Mentor Urban Planner: *Karen Heit*
Place Urban Planner's Office
Project Action Plan

Components

Pupil's Editions & Teacher's Editions

Literacy Place Kindergarten
provides a rich learning environment including Big Books, Read Alouds, Sentence Strips, Audiocassettes, Phonics Manipulatives, Workbooks, Teacher Editions, and much more.

Grades 1-5
▶ Literacy Place brings you what you would expect from Scholastic—authentic, award-winning children's literature.

▶ Our Teacher's Editions are easy to use, and provide explicit skills instruction.

▶ You'll also find a management CD-ROM to help you customize instruction to state and district standards.

scholastic.com
Check it out! You'll find a wealth of professional support resources, plus a lot of great stuff for kids and parents.

Pupil's Editions   **Teacher's Editions**

Support Materials

Practice
Literacy Place includes comprehensive practice resources.

- ✔ My Reading Workbook (1)
- ✔ Workshop and Project Cards (K-2)
- ✔ Practice Books (1-5)
- ✔ Spelling Resource Book (1-5)
- ✔ Grammar Resource Book (1-5)
- ✔ Handwriting Practice Book (K-3)
- ✔ ESL/ELD Resource Book (K-5)
- ✔ Skills Overhead Transparencies (2-5)
- ✔ Vocabulary Overhead Transparencies (2-5)
- ✔ Place Cards (3-5)

Assessment
Literacy Place provides a wide range of assessment and evaluation options. (K-5)

- ✔ Placement Tests
- ✔ Assessment Handbook
- ✔ Classroom Management Forms
- ✔ Selection Tests (for every story!)
- ✔ Unit Tests (Forms A and B)
- ✔ Oral Reading Assessment
- ✔ Scholastic Reading Inventory
- ✔ TAAS Preparation and Practice Book
- ✔ Assessment System CD-ROM

Technology
We set the industry standard.

- ✔ Phonics Practice CD-ROM (K-2)
- ✔ WiggleWorks Plus CD-ROM (K-2)
- ✔ Smart Place CD-ROM (3-5)
- ✔ Scholastic Management Suite (K-5)
- ✔ Staff Development Videos (K-5)
- ✔ Meet the Mentor Videos (K-5)
- ✔ Scholastic Network (K-5)
- ✔ Selection Audiocassettes (1-5)
- ✔ Classroom Resources CD-ROM (K-5)

Scholastic Solutions
Only Scholastic can offer you the diverse range of materials you need for your classroom. Please call 1-800-Scholastic for a catalog. Ask about these exciting products:

- ✔ High-Frequency Readers (K-1)
- ✔ Sound and Letter Books (K-1)
- ✔ Big Books/Little Books (K-2)
- ✔ Phonemic Awareness Kit (K-2)
- ✔ Phonics Readers (K-3)
- ✔ Phonics Chapter Books (1-3)
- ✔ Phonics Workbooks (K-2)

- ✔ Guided Reading Program (K-5)
- ✔ Bilingual Support (K-5)
- ✔ Solares (K-5)
- ✔ Transition Program (3-6)
- ✔ Sprint Plus Intervention (3-6)
- ✔ READ 180 (4-8)
- ✔ Reading Counts! (K-8)

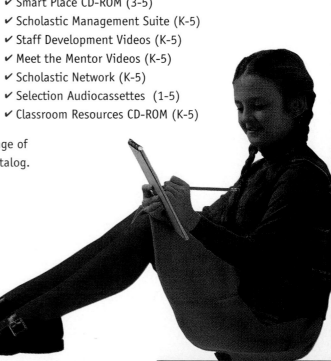

Advisors

Program Consultants

SKILLS, STRATEGIES, INSTRUCTION
James Bauman
Professor, University of Georgia,
Athens, Georgia

PHONICS AND EARLY READING
Wiley Blevins
Consultant and Educational Writer
New York, New York

ESL/ELD
Jacqueline Kiraithe-Cordova
Professor, California State, California

STAFF DEVELOPMENT
Nancy Cummings
Western Director of Implementation
Success For All School Restructuring
Phoenix, Arizona

BILINGUAL EDUCATION
James Cummins
Professor, Ontario Institute for
Studies in Education
Ontario, Canada

EARLY LITERACY DEVELOPMENT
Nell K. Duke
Michigan State University

ASSESSMENT/WRITING
Adele Fiderer
Consultant and Educational Writer
Scarsdale, New York

HANDWRITING
Steve Graham
Professor, University of Maryland
College Park, Maryland

WRITING
Shelley Harwayne
Director of Manhattan New School
New York, New York

SPELLING
Richard E. Hodges
Professor, University of Puget Sound
Tacoma, Washington

SPELLING
Louisa Moats
County Office of Education
Sacramento, California

VOCABULARY
William E. Nagy
Assistant Professor, University of Illinois
Champaign-Urbana, Illinois

FLEXIBLE GROUPING
Michael Opitz
Professor, University of Colorado
Boulder, Colorado

ESL/ELD
Robert Parker
Consultant, Brown University
Providence, Rhode Island

ESL/ELD
Cao Anh Quan
ESOL Program Specialist
Tallahassee, Florida

ESL/ELD
Kim Quan Nguyen-Lam
California State University
Long Beach, California

WRITING
Michael Strickland
Author, Consultant
Orange, New Jersey

Teacher Reviewers

Kim Andrews
Fourth Grade Reviewer
Baltimore, Maryland

Shirley Beard
Fourth Grade Reviewer
El Paso, Texas

Barbara Bloom
Fifth Grade Reviewer
Wall Lake, Iowa

Sherry Brown
Third Grade Reviewer
Georgetown, Texas

Lisa Buchholz
First Grade Reviewer
Wheaton, Illinois

Kathy Burdick
Fifth Grade Reviewer
Austin, Texas

Marianne Chorba
Fourth Grade Reviewer
Baltimore, Maryland

Peggy Colley
Third Grade Reviewer
Rocky Face, Georgia

Carol Curry
Third Grade Reviewer
Tallahassee, Florida

Claire Dale
First Grade Reviewer
National City, California

Mildred DeStefano
First Grade Reviewer
Brooklyn, New York

Doris Dillan
Grade Two Reviewer
San Jose, California

Oneaster Drummer
First Grade Reviewer
Cincinnati, Ohio

Ethel Durham
Third Grade Reviewer
Grand Rapids, Michigan

Patty Ernst
Second Grade Reviewer
Naples, New York

Alzada Fowler
First Grade Reviewer
Lake Helen, Florida

Jane Ginn
First Grade Reviewer
Rohnert Park, California

Amy Gordon
Third Grade Reviewer
New City, New York

Janet Gray
Fourth Grade Reviewer
Lake Helen, Florida

Velma Gunn
Fourth Grade Reviewer
New Rochelle, New York

Annie Ruth Harris
Third Grade Reviewer
Decatur, Alabama

Barbara Ann Hawkins
Second Grade Reviewer
Hamer, South Carolina

Amy Hom
Second Grade Reviewer
New York, New York

Min Hong
First Grade Reviewer
Brooklyn, New York

Susan Howe
Third Grade Reviewer
Ellicott City, Maryland

Barbara Jansz
First Grade Reviewer
Naperville, Illinois

Michele Jessen
First Grade Reviewer
El Paso, Texas

Ellen W. Johnson
Second Grade Reviewer
Chalfont, Pennsylvania

Vera Johnson
First Grade Reviewer
Uniondale, New York

Carol Kaiser
Third Grade Reviewer
Los Angeles, California

Karen Kolsky
Third Grade Reviewer
Philadelphia, Pennsylvania

Judy Keyak
Second Grade Reviewer
St. Petersburg, Florida

Jacqueline Krass
Second Grade Reviewer
Gulfport, Mississippi

Warren Livesley
Fourth Grade Reviewer
New York, New York

Libby Lesley
First Grade Reviewer
San Angelo, Texas

Dora I. Magana
Fourth Grade Reviewer
El Paso, Texas

Tim Mason
Second Grade Reviewer
Willington Florida

Carol Mercer
Fourth Grade Reviewer
National City, California

Betty Milburn
Third Grade Reviewer
Grand Prairie, Texas

Jane Moore
Third Grade Reviewer
Dallas, Texas

Sandy Nolan
Third Grade Reviewer
Salem, Wisconsin

Carol Ochs
Fifth Grade Reviewer
Noble, Oklahoma

Lynn Olson
Fifth Grade Reviewer
Omaha, Nebraska

Cynthia Orange
Second Grade Reviewer
Bronx, New York

Sue Panek
Fourth Grade Reviewer
Hawthorne, New Jersey

Deborah Peale
Fourth Grade Reviewer
Miami, Florida

Arturo Perez
Second Grade Reviewer
Ventura, California

Jeanette Reber
First Grade Reviewer
Rock Hill, South Carolina

Charlene Richardson
Fourth Grade Reviewer
Everett, Washington

Daria Rigney
Fifth Grade Reviewer
Brooklyn, New York

Andrea Ruff
First Grade Reviewer
Brooklyn, New York

Carol Shirmang
First Grade Reviewer
Palatine, Illinois

Wendy Smiley
Fourth Grade Reviewer
Syracuse, New York

Barbara Solomon
Second Grade Reviewer
Hempstead, New York

Alicia Sparkman
First Grade Reviewer
Plant City, Florida

Elaine Steinberg
Third Grade Reviewer
Fresh Meadows, New York

Bobby Stern
Third Grade Reviewer
Winston-Salem, North Carolina

Laura Stewart
First Grade Reviewer

Kate Taylor
Fifth Grade Reviewer
Baltimore, Maryland

Vasilika Terss
Second Grade Reviewer
St. Louis, Missouri

Linda Thorn
Fifth Grade Reviewer
Cranford, New Jersey

Gayle Thurn
Second Grade Reviewer
Piedmont, South Carolina

Jerry Trotter
Fifth Grade Reviewer
Chicago, Illinois

Julia Tucker
First Grade Reviewer
Hampton, Virginia

Patricia Viales
First Grade Reviewer
Salinas, California

Janielle Wagstaff
Second Grade Reviewer
Salt Lake City, Utah

Gail Weber
Fourth Grade Reviewer
Sherman Oaks, California

Elizabeth White
First Grade Reviewer
Bronx, New York

Karla Hawkins-Windeline
Second Grade Reviewer
Hickman, Nebraska

National Advisory Council

Barbara R. Foorman, Ph. D.
Professor of Pediatrics
Director of the Center for
Academic and Reading Skills
Houston, TX

Dr. Wilmer Cody
Commissioner of Education
Kentucky State Department
of Education
Frankfort, KY

Ms. Judy Mountjoy
Vice President
The National PTA
Chicago, IL

Ms. Anne Bryant
Executive Director
National School Boards
Association
Alexandria, VA

Dr. Anthony Alvarado
Chancellor for Instruction
San Diego City Schools
San Diego, CA

TEACHER'S EDITION

SCHOLASTIC

LITERACY PLACE®

UNIT 2

See It, Solve It

LITERACY PLACE AUTHORS

CATHY COLLINS BLOCK
Professor, Curriculum and Instruction, Texas Christian University

LINDA B. GAMBRELL
Professor, Education, University of Maryland at College Park

VIRGINIA HAMILTON
Children's Author; Winner of the Newbery Medal, the Coretta Scott King Award and the Laura Ingalls Wilder Lifetime Achievement Award

DOUGLAS K. HARTMAN
Associate Professor of Language and Literacy, University of Pittsburgh

TED S. HASSELBRING
Co-Director of the Learning Technology Center and Professor in the Department of Special Education at Peabody College, Vanderbilt University

ADRIA KLEIN
Professor, Reading and Teacher Education, California State University at San Bernardino

HILDA MEDRANO
Dean, College of Education, University of Texas-Pan American

GAY SU PINNELL
Professor, School of Teaching and Learning, College of Education, Ohio State University

D. RAY REUTZEL
Provost/Academic Vice President, Southern Utah University

DAVID ROSE
Founder and Executive Director of the Center for Applied Special Technology (CAST); Lecturer, Harvard University Graduate School of Education

ALFREDO SCHIFINI
Professor, School of Education, Division of Curriculum Instruction, California State University, Los Angeles

DELORES STUBBLEFIELD SEAMSTER
Principal, N.W. Harllee Elementary, Dallas, Texas; Consultant on Effective Programs for Urban Inner City Schools

QUALITY QUINN SHARP
Author and Teacher-Educator, Austin, Texas

JOHN SHEFELBINE
Professor, Language and Literacy Education, California State University at Sacramento

GWENDOLYN Y. TURNER
Associate Professor of Literacy Education, University of Missouri at St. Louis

Acknowledgments and credits appear on pages R28–R29, which constitute an extension of this copyright page.
Copyright © 2000 by Scholastic Inc.   All rights reserved.   Published by Scholastic Inc.   Printed in the U.S.A.

ISBN 0-439-07878-4 (National)

SCHOLASTIC, SCHOLASTIC LITERACY PLACE, and associated logos and designs are trademarks and/or registered trademarks of Scholastic Inc.

3 4 5 6 7 8 9 10   14   07 06 05 04 03 02 01 00

TABLE OF CONTENTS

See It, Solve It

We see problems and find solutions.

What's in Front?

What's in Back?

WEEKS 1 AND 2

WEEK 1

WEEK 2

WEEKS 3 AND 4

WEEK 3

WEEK 4

WEEKS 5 AND 6

WEEK 5

WEEK 6

Kindergarten Place at a Glance

PERSONAL VOICE
Stories About Us
We listen to, tell, and create stories.

WEEKS 1 AND 2

 All I Am
by Eileen Roe

Chrysanthemum
by Kevin Henkes

Quick as a Cricket
by Audrey Wood

WIGGLEWORKS PLUS: **Miss Mary Mack**

WEEKS 3 AND 4

 Coco Can't Wait!
by Taro Gomi

Pablo's Tree
by Pat Mora

Darlene
by Eloise Greenfield

········· STORYTELLING ·········
The Knee-High Man

WEEKS 5 AND 6

 I Like Books
by Anthony Browne

I Like Me!
by Nancy Carlson

The Little Red Hen
by Paul Galdone

WIGGLEWORKS PLUS:
What Lila Loves

PROBLEM SOLVING
See It, Solve It
We see problems and find solutions.

WEEKS 1 AND 2

 What Am I?
by N.N. Charles

The Three Bears
by Paul Galdone

Where's My Teddy?
by Jez Alborough

WIGGLEWORKS PLUS: **Birds on Stage**

WEEKS 3 AND 4

 I Went Walking
by Sue Williams

Caps for Sale
by Esphyr Slobodkina

Carlos and the Squash Plant
by Jan Romero Stevens

WIGGLEWORKS PLUS: **Boots**

WEEKS 5 AND 6

 Is Your Mama a Llama?
by Deborah Guarino

Corduroy
by Don Freeman

Anansi the Spider: A Tale from the Ashanti
by Gerald McDermott

········· STORYTELLING ·········
The Three Billy Goats Gruff

TEAMWORK
All Together Now!
We share and help each other.

WEEKS 1 AND 2

 The 100th Day of School
by Angela Shelf Medearis

Herman the Helper
by Robert Kraus

The Cow That Went OINK
by Bernard Most

WIGGLEWORKS PLUS: **Tortillas**

WEEKS 3 AND 4

 Jamberry
by Bruce Degen

Jamaica Tag-Along
by Juanita Havill

The Story of Chicken Licken
by Jan Ormerod

········· STORYTELLING ·········
The Great Big Enormous Turnip

WEEKS 5 AND 6

 Pizza Party!
by Grace Maccarone

Blueberries for Sal
by Robert McCloskey

Sione's Talo
by Lino Nelisi

WIGGLEWORKS PLUS: **Pizza**

PHONOLOGICAL AWARENESS

ABC Song, Names, Alphabetic Knowledge

A Was Once An Apple Pie
by Edward Lear

- **Mentor:** Honey Wada, a grandmother
- **Place:** Storytelling Corner

PHONOLOGICAL AWARENESS PHONICS

A B C D E F

Apples, Alligators and also Alphabets
by Odette and Bruce Johnson

- **Mentor:** Becky Wible, a claymator
- **Place:** Claymator's Studio

PHONOLOGICAL AWARENESS PHONICS

G H I J K L

Eating the Alphabet: Fruits and Vegetables from A to Z
by Lois Ehlert

- **Mentor:** Kwaku Twumasi, a pizza chef
- **Place:** Restaurant

CREATIVE EXPRESSION

Express Yourself
We express ourselves through songs, sounds, stories, dance, and art.

WEEKS 1 AND 2

 Listen to the Desert
by Pat Mora

A-Hunting We Will Go!
by Steven Kellogg

Mouse Mess
by Linnea Riley

 WIGGLEWORKS PLUS:
Let's Get the Rhythm

WEEKS 3 AND 4

 The Itsy Bitsy Spider
by Iza Trapani

The Three Little Pigs
by Gavin Bishop

Mama Zooms
by Jane Cowen-Fletcher

WIGGLEWORKS PLUS:
Clifford the Big Red Dog

WEEKS 5 AND 6

 Good-Night, Owl!
by Pat Hutchins

Minerva Louise at School
by Janet Morgan Stoeke

Whistle for Willie
by Ezra Jack Keats

.... STORYTELLING ....
The Spider Weaver

MANAGING INFORMATION

I Spy!
Information is all around us.

WEEKS 1 AND 2

 Nature Spy
by Shelley Rotner and
Ken Kreisler

Mice Squeak, We Speak
by Tomie dePaola

What Joe Saw
by Anna Grossnickle Hines

.... STORYTELLING ....
The Coyote and the Turtle

WEEKS 3 AND 4

 From Head to Toe
by Eric Carle

Over on the Farm
by Christopher Gunson

Foal
photographed by Gordon Clayton

 WIGGLEWORKS PLUS:
A Tree Can Be...

WEEKS 5 AND 6

 Flower Garden
by Eve Bunting

I Am the Peach
by Luisa de Noriega

The Tale of Peter Rabbit
by Beatrix Potter

 WIGGLEWORKS PLUS: **My Garden**

COMMUNITY INVOLVEMENT

Join In!
We help our community.

WEEKS 1 AND 2

 My River
by Shari Halpern

Time to Sleep
by Denise Fleming

Rosie's Walk
by Pat Hutchins

.... STORYTELLING ....
The Rabbit and the Elephant

WEEKS 3 AND 4

 **What the Sun Sees,
What the Moon Sees**
by Nancy Tafuri

Abuela
by Arthur Dorros

The Little House
by Virginia Lee Burton

 WIGGLEWORKS PLUS: **City Sounds**

WEEKS 5 AND 6

 Hattie and the Fox
by Mem Fox

Madeline's Rescue
by Ludwig Bemelmans

Officer Buckle and Gloria
by Peggy Rathmann

 WIGGLEWORKS PLUS:
Music Is in the Air

Phonics
PHONOLOGICAL AWARENESS PHONICS

M N O P Q R -an, -op

Alphabatics
by Suse MacDonald

- **Mentor:** Pat Mora,
  an author
- **Place:** Author's Studio

Phonics
PHONOLOGICAL AWARENESS PHONICS

S T U V W X -at, -un, -ig

Amazon Alphabet
by Martin and Tanis Jordan

- **Mentor:** Steven Powell,
  a farmer
- **Place:** Gardening Center

Phonics
PHONOLOGICAL AWARENESS PHONICS

Y Z -en, -ot, CVC words

ABCDrive!
by Naomi Howland

- **Mentor:** Tom Chapin,
  a singer
- **Place:** Performance Stage

CLAYMATOR'S STUDIO
SETTING UP THE PLACE

Why a Claymator's Studio?

"Making a piece of animation is like putting together a puzzle."

Becky Wible

Create a Workplace Model

Turn an art space into a claymator's studio filled with tools, supplies, and reference materials to allow for plenty of exploration. Encourage children to use problem solving and to use inventive thinking to discover solutions to problems.

View the Mentor Video

Ask children if they have ever seen a movie, show, or commercial that used clay. Have children describe how they think the clay characters are made. Then tell them that they are going to watch a video about a woman named Becky Wible who makes claymation movies. Explain that there are lots of problems that need to be solved to make a movie with clay. Invite children to watch the video to see how Becky and the people she works with solve problems.

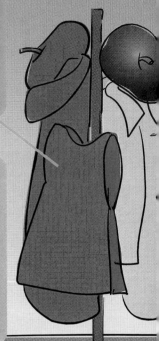

Artist's Clothing Rack

A coat rack can be used to hold artist's smocks, caps, and other special work clothing.

Reference Library

Set up an artist's reference library. Include information books, children's pictures, and storybooks in the collection to inspire young artists.

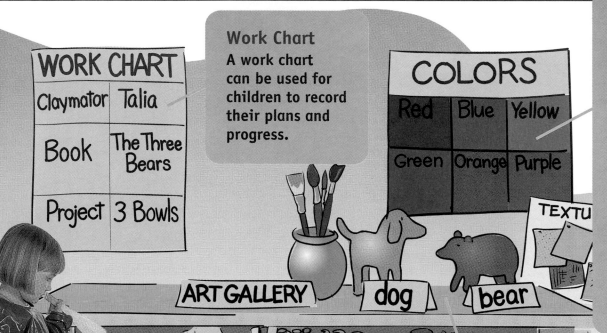

Work Chart
A work chart can be used for children to record their plans and progress.

WORK CHART

Claymator	Talia
Book	The Three Bears
Project	3 Bowls

Color Chart
Display a color chart that shows the clay colors and their names. A texture chart can also be displayed for added inspiration! Glue texture squares on a chart and label with texture words such as *bumpy, rough,* and *smooth.*

COLORS

| Red | Blue | Yellow |
| Green | Orange | Purple |

ART GALLERY dog bear

TEXTU

Exhibit Area
Make an exhibit area for children to display their finished creations. Provide markers, paper, and tape so that children can make gallery labels for the work that will be on display.

Supply Shelf
Provide a supply shelf stocked with colored clay and assorted tools, as well as shoe boxes, cardboard, and paints for backgrounds and bases. Store clay in containers labeled by color. Tools can include hammers, clay cutters, forks, a garlic press, a comb, and rolling pins.

WEEKS
1 AND 2

Kindergarten Goals
for Weeks 1 and 2

Oral Language/ Vocabulary

- participating in rhymes, songs, conversations, and discussions
- participating in choral readings
- exploring opposites, shape words, and size words
- exploring story vocabulary

Reading

- building alphabetic knowledge
- participating in shared reading
- engaging in emergent reading
- exploring concepts of print
- sequencing story events
- using picture clues
- using punctuation marks
- reading riddles
- reading high-frequency words

Writing

- making a picture word chart
- writing question marks
- writing letters: *Aa, Bb*
- illustrating and labeling opposites
- making a Big Book of Riddles
- writing word cards
- writing a lost-and-found poster
- engaging in shared writing
- writing independently in Journals
- writing a language-experience chart

Listening/Speaking/ Viewing

- listening responsively to texts read aloud
- identifying repetitive text
- listening for words relating to size
- identifying rhyming words
- developing phonological awareness
- sharing riddles
- presenting dramatic interpretations of stories
- singing songs
- engaging in conversations
- relating personal experiences to literature
- demonstrating visual literacy

Daily Phonics: *Aa* and *Bb*

- reciting classic poems, songs, and nursery rhymes
- naming and recognizing the letters
- recognizing sound/letter relationships
- generating words that begin with /a/, /b/
- decoding words using beginning sounds

Center Workshops and Project

- acquiring world knowledge through cross-curricular activities
- telling a story with clay

WEEKS 1 AND 2 RESOURCES

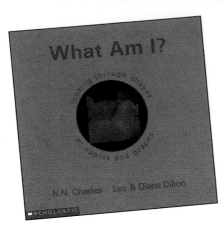

Big Book

Meet the Author
N.N. Charles earned a degree in creative writing and also studied design.

Meet the Illustrators
Leo and Diane Dillon have worked together for 30 years. They illustrated *Why Mosquitoes Buzz in People's Ears* and other books.

Available as audiocassette

Big Book of Rhymes and Rhythms

For teaching phonological awareness, the alphabet, and concepts of print.

- **"You Shall Have an Apple"**
- **"Baa, Baa, Black Sheep"**

Available as audiocassette

Read Aloud

Meet the Author/ Illustrator
Paul Galdone was born in Hungary and moved to the United States as a teenager. He wrote and illustrated 26 children's books and illustrated more than 100 books of other authors.

Read Aloud

Meet the Author/ Illustrator
Jez Alborough likes to draw and write about animals. He looks for photos of animals in books and sometimes goes to the zoo. His other books include *Clothesline, Cuddly Dudley,* and *Hide and Seek.*

ABC Book

Meet the Authors/ Illustrators
Bruce Johnson co-authored and illustrated three children's books with his daughter Odette. Bruce worked as a commercial artist. Odette Johnson creates clay animation for television. They used both skills to create *Apples, Alligators and also Alphabets.*

Side One

Side Two

SourceCard

- What do the signs say?
- "The Wheels on the Bus"

High-Frequency Reader

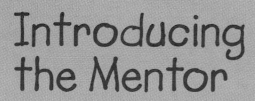

My Read and Write Book

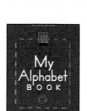

My Alphabet Book

ESL/ELD Teaching Guide

My Books

To take home to share.

Introducing the Mentor

Becky Wible turns words into pictures, pictures into clay, and clay into movies! In other words, she's an animator. Becky solves problems every day, just as kindergartners do. She asks questions, answers questions, and finds new solutions.

DAYS AT A GLANCE

WEEKS 1 AND 2

	Daily Phonics	Literature	Shared Writing	Workshops and Projects
DAY 1	Phonological Awareness: Alliteration Syllables	***Apples, Alligators and also Alphabets*** by Odette and Bruce Johnson	Make an ABC Picture Chart	Alphabet: Sort Aa's and Bb's Art: Set Up the Claymator's Studio
DAY 2	**Vowel /a/a** Phonological Awareness: Oral Segmentation: Beginning Sounds	***What Am I?*** by N.N. Charles illustrated by Leo and Diane Dillon	Focus on Questions	Math: What Am I? Art: Our Fruit
DAY 3	**Vowel /a/a** Phonological Awareness: Alliteration Introduce Sound-Spelling	***What Am I?*** by N.N. Charles **High-Frequency Reader:** *I Am*	Concepts of Print: Words and Sentences Write *Aa* Write Class Book	Listening: Who Am I? Art: Still Life
DAY 4	**Vowel /a/a** Phonological Awareness: Syllables Review Sound-Spelling	***The Three Bears*** by Paul Galdone	Illustrate and Label Opposites	Math: What Would Goldilocks Do? Art: Bear-o-Ramas
DAY 5	**Vowel /a/a** Phonological Awareness: Rhyme Maintain Sound-Spelling	**"You Shall Have an Apple"** a poem *Apples, Alligators and also Alphabets* **My Book:** *Who Is Ben?*	Concepts of Print: Words that Begin with *Aa* High-Frequency Words: *am*	Games: What Am I? Alphabet: *Aa* is For . . .

	Daily Phonics	Literature	Shared Writing	Workshops and Projects
DAY 6	**Consonant /b/b** Phonological Awareness: Oral Segmentation	*Birds on Stage* by Saturnino Romay	Make a Big Book of Riddles	Science: Bird Watch Art: Clay Birds
DAY 7	**Consonant /b/b** Phonological Awareness: Oddity Task Introduce Sound-Spelling	**SourceCard** What Do the Signs Say? "The Wheels on the Bus" **High-Frequency Reader:** *I Am*	Make Word Cards Write *Bb*	Art: Drawing Signs Blocks: Our Town
DAY 8	**Consonant /b/b** Phonological Awareness: Oral Blending Review Sound-Spelling	*Where's My Teddy?* by Jez Alborough READ ALOUD	Make a Lost-and-Found Poster	Science: Bears' Beds Art: Plenty of Prints
DAY 9	**Consonant /b/b** Phonological Awareness: Oral Segmentation Maintain Sound-Spelling	"Baa, Baa, Black Sheep" a rhyme *Apples, Alligators and also Alphabets* **My Book:** *Hair*	Concepts of Print: Connect Speaking and Writing	Alphabet: *Bb* Finger Fun Art: Our Beautiful Bears
DAY 10	Phonological Awareness: Alliteration Phonics Maintenance	**Review Books from Weeks 1 and 2**	Make a Compare and Contrast Language Chart	Project: Tell a Story With Clay

DAY 1 OBJECTIVES

CHILDREN WILL:

- listen for alliteration
- recognize *Aa, Bb*
- read *Apples, Alligators and also Alphabets*
- clap syllables
- categorize words by ABC's
- make a sound/letter chart
- use picture clues
- engage in Center Workshops

MATERIALS

- *Apples, Alligators and also Alphabets*
- Picture cards, R33–34

GUIDED READING

To conclude each day's reading session, meet with guided reading groups. You might use Scholastic's Guided Reading Library or other books in your library.

Share the ABC Book

DAILY PHONICS

Warm-Up: Wordplay

PHONOLOGICAL AWARENESS

Alex and Alice Read this alliterative sentence aloud, stressing each initial /a/ sound: *Alex and Alice picked apples*. Invite children to repeat the sentence and then to tell you what is alike about the words. Help them recognize that most of the words in the sentence begin with the same sound—/a/.

Word Parts Clap each syllable as you say *apple*. Ask children to count the number of times you clap as you say the word again. Explain that each clap stands for one part, or syllable, of the word. Say some words aloud; have children repeat each word and clap and count the number of parts in the word.

| apron | alligator | ape | acorn | alphabet | ant |

Build Background

ORAL LANGUAGE: CATEGORIZE BY ABC'S

Show picture cards of objects whose names begin with *Bb*: *bat, bee, bus*. Ask volunteers to name the pictures. Then ask children to identify what the pictures have in common. Place the picture cards together where children can see them.

Repeat the process with picture cards for *Cc* and *Dd*. Point out that we can find things grouped by their first letter in many places. Give examples such as books in libraries and words in the dictionary and in the alphabet book they are about to read.

PREVIEW AND PREDICT

Display the cover of *Apples, Alligators and also Alphabets*, reading the title and the authors' names.

► **Can you name the animals on the cover? What clues do you see that tell you this is an ABC book?**

► **Why do you think these things are together on the cover?**

Read the ABC Book

ALPHABETIC KNOWLEDGE: *Aa* AND *Bb*

Open *Apples, Alligators and also Alphabets* to the *Aa* page. Point out the large capital and small *Aa*. Ask children to look for another capital *A* in the illustration. Then turn to the *Bb* page and point to the capital and small *Bb*.

Read each page, inviting children to name the objects they see. Help them understand that the name of objects on each page begin with the same letter. Help children with difficult vocabulary by pointing to the pictures as you say them. Encourage children to predict the letters that will appear on the following page.

Respond to the Literature

TALK ABOUT IT

Share Personal Responses Encourage children to share their personal responses to the book. Remind children that they already know a book like *Apples, Alligators and also Alphabets*.

▶ **How is this book like *A Was Once an Apple Pie*? How is it different?**

▶ **What was your favorite page of *Apples, Alligators and also Alphabets*?**

THINK ABOUT IT

Focus on *Aa* and *Bb* Look at the *Aa* page and ask a volunteer to point to pictures whose names begin with *Aa*. Then turn to the *Bb* page. Point to the letters and the bubbles, balloons, and baboons in the illustration. Help children see that many of the picture names begin with **/b/**.

▶ **What other things do you see in the picture that begin with the same sound?**

Guide children to look for pictures whose names begin with the same sounds on other pages in the book.

Apples, Alligators
and also
Alphabets

Odette and Bruce Johnson

Apples, Alligators and also Alphabets

EXTRA HELP

■ Invite children to choose a letter. Help them think of things that begin with that letter sound. Invite them to draw a picture. Collect their drawings and make an alphabet book or alphabet bulletin board. **(CATEGORIZE)**

TEACHER TIP
Before rereading an ABC Book, I always preview the book and draw children's attention to the order of the letters.

MODIFY Instruction

EXTRA HELP

■ Provide children with magnetic letters or letter cards for each letter of the alphabet. Help children use the ABC book, *Apples, Alligators and also Alphabets*, to help them put the letters in ABC order. **(SEQUENCE)**

Shared Writing

MAKE AN ABC PICTURE CHART

Look through *Apples, Alligators and Also Alphabets* with children and focus on the illustrations. Guide children to see that there are many pictures on each page that have names that begin with the same sound.

- Have children turn to the *Cc* page; read the words on the page. Then ask children to look for other pictures on the page whose names begin with the same sound.
- Together make a *Cc* chart. Write the words that children name on the chart. Invite volunteers to help you write using the letters that they know.
- Children may want to illustrate words on the chart. Repeat this exercise on other pages in the book.

Repeated Reading

USE PICTURE CLUES

Reread the book with children. Invite them to help you read the words by pointing to the picture clue. Encourage children to talk about what is happening in the illustrations on each page.

READ AND WRITE INDEPENDENTLY

Journal Invite children to reread *Apples, Alligators and also Alphabets* on their own or in small groups. Children can write or draw in their Journals about their favorite letter page.

✅ Comprehension Check

ACT IT OUT

As you reread the ABC book, children can act out something they see on each page. For example, children may act like an alligator with an apple in its mouth. Classmates can guess what is being acted out.

HOME/SCHOOL CONNECTION

Give children the Family Newsletter from My Read and Write Book to bring home. Read the Newsletter to children and talk about what it says. Discuss what children will do in school and what they will say to their parents.

CENTER WORKSHOPS

MATERIALS

- *Aa* and *Bb* Alphabet manipulatives
- *Aa* and *Bb* ABC Cards
- Two sorting trays such as baskets
- Paper plates or boxes, labeled "Aa" and "Bb"

Sort *Aa*'s and *Bb*'s!

Place your *Aa* and *Bb* ABC Cards in a visible spot. From your classroom supplies, set out a collection of alphabet manipulatives such as alphabet puzzle pieces, magnetic letters, sponge letters, or felt letter cutouts.

Using the ABC Cards as a reference, encourage children to sort out *Aa* and *Bb* manipulatives and to place them on a labeled sorting tray or basket.

Observation: How do children use the ABC Cards as they sort the items?

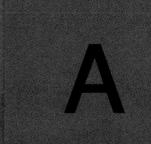

MATERIALS

- Clay
- *Aa* and *Bb* ABC Cards
- Butcher paper

Set Up the Claymator's Studio

Introduce children to the claymator's studio. Remind them of the studio in the Meet the Mentor Video. Point out that the illustrations in *Apples, Alligators and also Alphabets* are made of clay.

- Explain that children will be working in the claymator's studio over the next few weeks. Encourage children to explore using the clay.
- Children can manipulate the clay to create "snakes." Using the rolled-out clay, they can form the letters *Aa* and *Bb*.
- Label two pieces of butcher paper "Aa" and "Bb." Let children display their creations on the papers.

Observation: Notice how children experiment using the clay.

DAY 2
OBJECTIVES

CHILDREN WILL:

- orally segment words (beginning sounds)
- recognize /a/
- read and respond to *What Am I?*
- explore riddles
- identify shapes
- identify question marks
- engage in Center Workshops

MATERIALS

- *What Am I?*
- **My Read and Write Book,** pp. 5–6

 The Big Book is available on audiocassette in the Literacy Place Listening Center. The song is available on the **Sounds of Phonics** audiocassette.

My Read and Write Book, p. 5

Share the Big Book

Vowel /a/a

PHONOLOGICAL AWARENESS

Oral Segmentation: Beginning Sounds Read the song title below. Ask what sound children hear at the beginning of *ant.*

- Invite children to repeat the word *ant* with you as you exaggerate the beginning sound—*a-a-a-ant.*
- Then sing the song. Invite children to sing along. Encourage them to emphasize the **/a/** sound in the word *ants.*

The Ants Came Marching

1. **The ants came marching one by one, Hurrah! Hurrah!**
   The ants came marching one by one
   The little one stopped to suck his thumb.
   They all go marching down around the town.
   (Boom, boom, boom)
2. **The ants came marching two by two...**
   The little one stopped to tie his shoe...

Build Background

ORAL LANGUAGE: SHAPES

Encourage children to name the shapes they know. Use pictures or objects shaped like circles, rectangles, squares, diamonds, etc. to generate a web of shape words. As you write each word, invite a volunteer to draw a picture of the shape. Encourage children to name objects in the classroom that have these shapes.

PREVIEW AND PREDICT

Explain that a riddle is a question that gives clues to an answer. Encourage children to share riddles they know.

Display the cover of *What Am I?* Read the title and the author's and illustrator's names, tracking the print.

▶ **What shapes do you see? What is inside them?**

▶ **What do you think the book is about?**

Read the Big Book

MAKE PREDICTIONS

Read the riddle on the first page of the book. Encourage children to try to predict the answer.

- Before you turn each page, encourage children to guess the answer to each riddle.
- Remind them to think about the color and other clues as well as the picture on the inside cover.
- Help children identify each shape they look through.

What Am I?

Respond to the Literature

TALK ABOUT IT

Share Personal Responses Encourage children to share their personal responses to the book.

▶ **What kinds of fruit did you see?**

▶ **Have you tasted these different fruits?**

▶ **What are your favorite fruits?**

Ask the children to describe the tastes of each fruit they have eaten.

THINK ABOUT IT

Using Picture Clues Talk together about the riddles in the book and how children were able to answer them.

▶ **What were the clues that the author gave to help you figure out what the fruit on the next page would be?**

▶ **Could you have told the answer just by looking through the shape? What else helped you?**

Read the poem on the first page of the book again and ask children if they can figure out the answer now.

MODIFY Instruction

ESL/ELD

▲ **English language learners may find riddles challenging because they require fluency in the language and familiarity with the culture. During the Build Background section, invite children acquiring English to share riddles in their first languages. Their classmates may enjoy listening to new riddles. (MAKE CONNECTIONS)**

OBSERVATION

How are children doing? Are they:

- distinguishing between a statement and a question?
- identifying words that rhyme?
- making predictions?

Keep the answers to these questions in mind when planning Day 3, Revisit the Big Book.

ESL/ELD

▲ Go over the names of the fruits and the colors featured in this story with English language learners before they try to participate in the group readings. **(STEP-BY-STEP)**

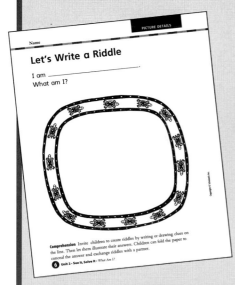

Name

Let's Write a Riddle

I am ——————
What am I?

Comprehension Invite children to create riddles by writing or drawing clues on the line. Then let them illustrate their answers. Children can fold the paper to conceal the answer and exchange riddles with a partner.

Unit 2 • See It, Solve It • *What Am I?*

**My Read and Write Book,
p. 6**

Shared Writing

FOCUS ON QUESTIONS

Show children the question "What Am I?" on the cover of the Big Book.

▶ **Have you ever seen this kind of sentence before?**

▶ **Have you ever seen this mark at the end of a sentence?**

- Write the question "Which one is your favorite?" at the top of a chart, leaving out the question mark.
- Read the question with children and ask them what is missing from the end of the sentence. Have a volunteer add the question mark.
- Ask children which fruits are their favorites. Write the names of the fruits together, asking children to write the first letter of the word they suggest. Children can add illustrations.

Repeated Reading

LISTEN FOR RHYMING WORDS

Reread the Big Book, pointing out the names of the fruits. Invite children to help you search for rhyming words such as *sweet, eat; thin, skin; nice, slice*. Remind children that words that rhyme sound alike at the end but have different beginnings.

READ AND WRITE INDEPENDENTLY

Journal Place copies of *What Am I?* in the Reading Center, along with the audiocassette. Encourage children to draw pictures of and write about their favorite fruits in their Journals.

✓ Comprehension Check

RETELL THE STORY

Whisper one of the following fruit names from the story in each child's ear: *apple, orange, banana, avocado, blueberry, grape*. Then have children take turns telling something about their fruit. Let the other children guess what fruit is being described.

CENTER WORKSHOPS

What Am I?

Provide a variety of cutout shapes, and help children name each shape. Encourage children to create objects by gluing the cutout shapes to a piece of paper and decorating them. Anything goes.

- Help children mount the shape objects onto a large butcher paper mural. Encourage children to name their creations and to write labels for each.

- Tape the labels to the mural, like hinges, with the words upside down and facing inward. Children can lift up the card to read the answer to the question "What am I?"

Observation: Notice how children use the shape clues to guess what the objects are.

MATERIALS

- Cutout shapes
- Construction paper
- Butcher paper
- Pencils
- Crayons, markers
- Scissors, glue
- Art scraps

Our Fruit

Display *What Am I?* opened to the picture of the collection of fruit on the inside cover. Invite children to choose a fruit to mold out of clay.

- Model how to use an etching tool to draw the diamonds on a pineapple. Then model how to roll and cut a piece of clay to form a leaf for an apple.

- Encourage children to explore other ways to make fruits. Place completed fruit on the tray labelled, "Our Fruit."

Observation: Which tools do children like to use? Which ones seem easier for them to manipulate?

MATERIALS

- *What Am I?*
- Colored clay
- Etching tools
- Clay hammers
- Plastic knives
- Tray

DAY 3 OBJECTIVES

CHILDREN WILL:

- listen for alliteration
- identify /a/a
- write *Aa*
- explore colors, shapes, fruits
- identify words and sentences
- identify high-frequency word: *am*
- read the High-Frequency Reader: *I Am*
- engage in Center Workshops

MATERIALS

- *Apples, Alligators and also Alphabets*
- *What Am I?*
- High-Frequency Reader: *I Am*
- My Alphabet Book, p. 3
- My Read and Write Book, p. 7

 The Big Book is available on audiocassette in the Literacy Place Listening Center.

My Alphabet Book, p. 3

DAILY PHONICS and Read the High-Frequency Reader

Vowel /a/a

Ⓐ PHONOLOGICAL AWARENESS

Alliteration Write the following alliterative sentence on the chalkboard: *Alice Alligator adds apples and apricots to applesauce.* Read the sentence aloud, stressing the initial sound. Ask children what sound they hear at the beginning of the words. Then have children repeat the sentence emphasizing the /a/ sound.

Ⓑ CONNECT SOUND-SPELLING

Introduce Vowel /a/a Open *Apples, Alligators and also Alphabets* to the **Aa** page. Point out to children that the letter **a** stands for /a/ as in **apples.**

- Ask children to say the sound with you.
- Point to the apple and say its name. Ask children to repeat *apple* and exaggerate the beginning sound /a/.

Letter Formation

WRITE THE LETTER

Write *Aa* on the chalkboard. Point out the capital and small forms of the letter. Model how to write the letter using the rhymes provided.

- Have children write both forms of the letter. Ask children to make the letter's sound as they practice writing.
- Note children's pencil grip and paper position.

A	a
Make a pointy hat, *(Slant down diagonally to the left, slant down diagonally to the right.)* Then wear it... That's that! *(Pull straight across.)*	Circle around and stop at the top, *(Curve around to the left and stop at the top.)* Then go straight down. That's where you stop. *(Pull straight down.)*

Reread the Big Book

OPTIONS

Colors and Shapes As you reread the Big Book, encourage children to name the colors and shapes in the illustrations. Talk together about other places children see these colors and shapes.

Fruits and Insects Encourage children to point to the name of each fruit as they reread *What Am I?*

▶ **Which of these fruits have you tasted?**

Ask children to name and describe the insects on each fruit page.

Story Message Read the text on the last page of the Big Book.

▶ **Why do you think the illustrator drew different hands? How are the hands different? How are they the same?**

▶ **What do you think the author means by "make the world a better place?"**

READ AND WRITE INDEPENDENTLY

Journal Place copies of *What Am I?* in the Reading Center for children to read independently or in small groups. In their Journals, children can draw fruits they like to eat and label each by name and color.

What Am I?

MODIFY Instruction

ESL/ELD

▲ Encourage English language learners to participate in this activity by modeling and then saying: *Point to a question mark. Show me a capital letter. Point to a word. Point to a period.* **(TOTAL PHYSICAL RESPONSE)**

Concepts of Print

EXPLORE WORDS AND SENTENCES

Display the first page of the Big Book and point to the words *red* and *square*. Then read the sentence aloud as you run your hands under each word. Explain that:

• a word is made up of letters.

• a sentence is made up of a group of words.

Then ask volunteers to look at the page and point to examples of words and sentences. Encourage them to read the words and the sentences.

Guide children to understand that a sentence is made up of words; it begins with a capital letter and ends with a period or question mark. Continue looking through the book, inviting volunteers to point out examples of words and sentences.

I Am

Written by Adria Klein
Illustrated by Susan Gal

SCHOLASTIC

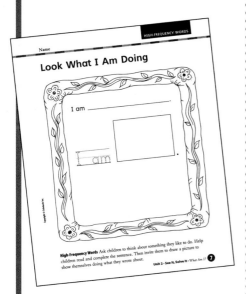

My Read and Write Book, p. 7

Read High-Frequency Reader

INTRODUCE THE BOOK

Show the book *I Am*. Read the title and the author's name. Explain that this book tells about the different things the girl on the cover is doing.

▶ **What are some things you like to do when you play?**

▶ **What do you think the girl on the cover will do?**

HIGH-FREQUENCY WORD: *am*

Write the sentence stem *I am* _____ on the board. Underline the word *am.* Then write the word *am* on a note card. Read it aloud.

• Display the card and have children read the word.

• Help children spell it aloud, clapping on each letter.

• Ask children to write it in the air as they state aloud each letter.

Review the high-frequency word *I* by asking a volunteer to find it on the Word Wall and read it aloud.

Invite children to complete the sentence stem by naming something they like to do at home such as reading, drawing, or playing. Write each new sentence on the board. Add the card for *am* to the Word Wall.

SHARE THE HIGH-FREQUENCY READER

Read the story aloud, tracking the print. Invite children to point to the high-frequency words *I* and *am.*

• After each two-page spread ask: *Can you do what the girl is doing?* Encourage children to tell about activities they enjoy.

SHARED WRITING

Invite the children to make a class book called *What Am I Doing?*

• Ask each child to think of an activity that they enjoy. Help children write and complete the sentence, *I am* _____ on a sheet of paper. Have them illustrate their sentence. Bind the pages into a book and share it with the class.

CENTER WORKSHOPS

Who Am I?

Invite children to think about what makes them special. Children can record their ideas onto an audiocassette. Each narrative should end with "Who am I?" You can model the activity for children by describing yourself. For example: *I have short brown hair and blue eyes. I like to play soccer and eat pizza. Who am I?*

- When everyone has had a turn, gather in a circle to listen to the tape. Children will have a lot of fun listening to themselves while their classmates try to guess who they are.

- Place the audiocassette in the Listening Center for further enjoyment.

Observation: What clues do children give to describe themselves? How do they guess which child is being described?

MATERIALS
- **Tape recorder**

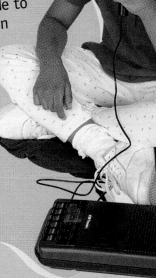

Still Life

Individuals To extend yesterday's activity in the claymator's studio, children can use black construction paper and colored chalk to make still-life drawings of the class fruit tray.

Observation: Notice the way children choose colors.

MATERIALS
- **Black construction paper**
- **Colored chalk**

Share the Read Aloud

DAY 4 OBJECTIVES

CHILDREN WILL:

- clap syllables
- review vowel /a/a
- listen and respond to *The Three Bears*
- name opposites
- discover repetitive structure
- sequence story events
- illustrate and label opposites
- engage in Center Workshops

MATERIALS

- *The Three Bears*
- ABC Card for *Aa*

Vowel /a/a

Ⓐ PHONOLOGICAL AWARENESS

Oral Segmentation: Syllables Clap each syllable as you say the name *Alex*. Ask children to count the number of times you clap as you say the word again. Then ask children to clap and count the number of parts in these words: *ant, apple, apricot, after, alligator, ago.*

Ⓑ CONNECT SOUND-SPELLING

An *Aa* Hunt Display the ABC Card for *Aa*, if available. Have children name the letter and the picture. Review that *a* stands for /a/ as in *apple*. Ask children to suggest words that begin with **/a/.** Write each word on the chalkboard, and have volunteers circle the letter ***a.***

Then invite partners to go on an *Aa* hunt to find *Aa*'s on book covers, posters, and artwork around the room.

Build Background

ORAL LANGUAGE: OPPOSITES

Hold up an eraser, feel the bottom of it and say *soft*. Then hold up a hardcover book, tap the cover and say *hard*. Then say the words *cold, big,* and *old,* and ask children to name the opposites.

- ▶ **Can you name things that are hot? cold?**
- ▶ **What are some things that are long? short?**

PREVIEW AND PREDICT

Show children the cover of *The Three Bears*. Read the title and the author/illustrator's name.

- ▶ **Do you recognize the name of this story?**
- ▶ **How are the three bears on the cover different?**

SET A PURPOSE

Ask children to listen for anything that is different about this retelling of *The Three Bears.*

Share the Read Aloud

DISCOVER REPETITIVE STRUCTURE

Read the story, adjusting the sound of your voice for the parts of the different-sized bears. Encourage children to guess which objects on each page belong to each bear.

Encourage children to predict which sized object Goldilocks will try next—the great big one, the medium-sized one, or the little wee one.

The Three Bears

Respond to the Literature

TALK ABOUT IT

Share Personal Responses Invite children to share their responses to the tale.

▶ **Which character did you like best? Why?**

▶ **What if Goldilocks had waited at the bears' house?**

▶ **Was the story the same or different from one you've heard before?**

Children might enjoy responding to *The Three Bears* by singing a song about bears such as "The Bear Went Over the Mountain."

THINK ABOUT IT

Focus on Sequence Ask children to think about the order in which events take place in the story.

▶ **Goldilocks tries everything in a certain order. Which size does she try first? Second? Third?**

▶ **What did the bears notice first? What did they notice next? What was the last thing the bears noticed?**

MODIFY Instruction

EXTRA HELP

■ Divide children into three groups: Great Big Bear, Medium-Sized Bear, and Little Wee Bear. As you read the story, invite each group to read their corresponding part with you. Remind children that they should adjust the level of their voices according to the size of the bear. **(READ ALOUD)**

PROFESSIONAL DEVELOPMENT

ADRIA KLEIN

Developing Oral Language Through Read Alouds

💡 *As children listen to quality literature read aloud, they become aware of the rhythm and sounds of oral language. Children will use this understanding as they develop early reading skills.*

MODIFY Instruction

ESL/ELD

▲ Provide children with a list of words and their meanings for the Shared Writing activity. Use words that are easily defined such as big/small. Model: *This is big, its opposite is small. Now you try it.* (MODEL)

Shared Writing

ILLUSTRATE AND LABEL OPPOSITES

Ask children to recall the words that describe the Medium-Sized Bear's and the Great Big Bear's porridge. (One was too hot, and one was too cold). Point out that the words *hot* and *cold* are opposites.

- Provide one word in pairs of opposites, for example: *hard, sad, hungry,* and *big.*
- Have children suggest words that mean the opposite. As they make suggestions, write them on the board.
- Ask each child to choose a pair of opposites and to draw pictures to illustrate the two words in the pair.
- Help children label their illustrations with the opposite words. Invite them to show their pictures and read the labels.

Repeated Reading

FOCUS ON CHARACTERS

Before you reread the story, encourage children to notice the different print sizes on the page.

▶ **Which bear is the storyteller writing about when he uses small print? medium print? large print?**

Invite children to join in as you read the repetitive text. Encourage them to change the sound level of their voices as they read to reflect the feelings of the characters.

▶ **How would the Great Big Bear sound if he was feeling grouchy? sad?**

▶ **How would the Medium-Sized Bear sound if she was angry?**

▶ **How would the Little Wee Bear sound if he was surprised? upset?**

READ AND WRITE INDEPENDENTLY

Journal Place *The Three Bears* in the Reading Center for children to read. Children can draw and write about another item that the bears might have, showing it in three different sizes.

✅ Comprehension Check

ACT IT OUT

Children can act out the story using simple props, such as three bowls for the porridge, three large blocks as chairs, and three blankets or towels for the beds.

CENTER WORKSHOPS

What Would Goldilocks Do?

Using a variety of manipulatives, set up and label trays so that children can sort materials by size.

- Label the trays as "big things," "medium-sized things," and "little wee things."

- Encourage children to sort the items by size and to recall the items in the story that were big, medium, and little.

Observation: How do children approach the problem and sort by size?

MATERIALS

- Manipulatives that can be sorted by size, such as screws, doll furniture, cubes, paper clips
- Trays, baskets, or paper plates for sorting

Bear-O-Ramas

Children can make bear dioramas by recreating a scene from the story using clay.

- Encourage children to form small groups and to select a scene from *The Three Bears* that they want to recreate.

- Give each group a shoebox, and encourage children to work together to make the objects.

- When the dioramas are finished, ask the children in each group to describe what is happening in the scene they have depicted. Write down responses on a card, and attach the card to their diorama.

Observation: Notice which scenes children choose and how they describe their dioramas.

MATERIALS

- Clay
- *The Three Bears*
- Clay hammer
- Etching tools
- Rolling pin
- Plastic knives
- Cards
- Shoeboxes

Baby Bear's chair is broken.

DAY 5 OBJECTIVES

CHILDREN WILL:

- read a rhyme
- review /a/a
- connect speaking and writing
- review high-frequency words
- read My Book: *Who Is Ben?*
- engage in Center Workshops

MATERIALS

- *Big Book of Rhymes and Rhythms,* p. 6
- **Sentence Strips for "You Shall Have an Apple"**
- **Pocket chart**
- *Apples, Alligators and also Alphabets*
- **My Book:** *Who Is Ben?*
- **My Read and Write Book,** p. 8

Read-Aloud Rhyme: Aa

You Shall Have an Apple

You shall have an apple,
You shall have a plum,
You shall have a rattle,
When papa comes home.

Make a rattle.
Use it as you say the rhyme.

Write the letters A and a.

Phonics Lead children in chanting the rhyme. Then let them use materials such as yogurt cups and margarine tubs to make rattles to accompany their chant. Children can take the rattles home.

Family Fun Say the ryhyme with your child using the rattles he or she made.

B Unit 2 - See It, Solve It · Vowel /a/ a

My Read and Write Book, p. 8

For additional practice see *Scholastic Phonics K,* pages 11–14. Also see Sound and Letter Book: *Ants.*

Sounds and Letters

DAILY PHONICS

and Read My Book

Vowel /a/a

A PHONOLOGICAL AWARENESS

Repetition Read aloud "You Shall Have an Apple" from the *Big Book of Rhymes and Rhythms.* Ask children what sound they hear at the beginning of the word *apple.* Then ask them to listen for the words that are repeated as you read the poem again, tracking the print. Help children see that *you shall have* is repeated four times.

Aa

You Shall Have an Apple
You shall have an apple,
You shall have a plum,
You shall have a rattle,
When papa comes home.

Big Book of Rhymes and Rhythms, p. 6

B CONCEPTS OF PRINT

Place the *Big Book of Rhymes and Rhythms,* the Sentence Strips for "You Shall Have an Apple," and a pocket chart in the Reading Center.

- Read "You Shall Have an Apple," asking children to clap in time with the rhythm.
- Reread the rhyme together. Ask volunteers to place the Sentence Strips in a pocket chart as you read each line.
- Have children frame each word in a sentence.
- Then have children point to the word that begins with *Aa.*

You shall have an apple,

You shall have a plum,

You shall have a rattle,

When papa comes home.

MODIFY
Instruction

ESL/ELD

▲ Encourage English language learners to act out each sentence written for the Vocabulary Activity to show that they understand it. (ACT IT OUT)

ⓒ CONNECT SOUND-SPELLING

Alphabetic Principle Remind children that the letter *a* stands for /a/ in *apple*. Display the cover of the ABC book *Apples, Alligators and also Alphabets* and let children find the words that begin with *Aa*. Encourage children to say the words with you as they find them, using the picture clues to help them.

ABC Book Explain to children that they are going to make a new page for their own ABC book. Have children suggest animals, objects, and people whose names begin with **/a/**. When the list is complete, invite children to work together to create the *Aa* page for their ABC Books.

Alphabet Center Place the ABC Book and the Big Book in the Alphabet Center. Also provide magnetic or cutout letters for *Aa*. Have children match the magnetic letters to those they find in the books.

ⓓ VOCABULARY: HIGH-FREQUENCY WORDS

Write the incomplete sentence *I am* _____ on the chalkboard. Read the sentence aloud and then do the following:

• Review each high-frequency word in the sentence. If necessary, review the read-spell-write routine.

• Write *hungry* in the blank space and read the sentence aloud. Invite children to act out the sentence.

• Ask each child to think of a word to replace *hungry* and to act out the new sentence. Let the other children guess the new word. Write it in the blank. Encourage children to read the sentence, pointing to each word as they read.

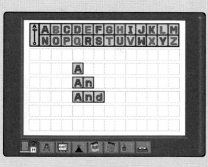

TECHNOLOGY

 Help children build words by asking them to write *A* on the **WiggleWorks Plus** Magnet Board. Ask children to add the letters *n,* and *nd* to make new words as shown above.

 The rhyme in the *Big Book of Rhymes and Rhythms* is available on the **Sounds of Phonics** audiocassette.

WHO IS BEN?

by Cass Hollander
Illustrated by Mavis Smith

■SCHOLASTIC

Who Is Ben?

EXTRA HELP

■ After children read about each clue that Ben draws, have them turn to page 8. Help them look at the teddy bear and find the part that Ben used in his drawing. **(PICTURE CLUES)**

Read My Book

INTRODUCE THE BOOK

Let children know that they are going to get their own book that they can read on their own and take home.

▶ **Is there a way to tell a riddle with pictures, not words? How could you do it?**

PREVIEW AND PREDICT

Pass out copies of *Who Is Ben?* Read the title and the author's and illustrator's names. Ask children about the illustration on the cover.

▶ **Whose eyes do you think these are?**

▶ **What do you think this book might be about?**

READ TOGETHER

Read the My Book with children, tracking the print as you read. Guide children to read along in their copies and to pay close attention to what the boy is drawing.

PHONICS

Ask children to say the word *bear* aloud.

▶ **What sound do you hear at the beginning of the word?**

READ AND WRITE INDEPENDENTLY

Journal Invite children to read *Who Is Ben?* on their own or in small groups. Encourage children to have a conversation with a partner about the boy in the story. Provide crayons and invite children to color the illustrations.

HOME/SCHOOL CONNECTION

Children can take home their My Books to share with family members and friends. Suggest that children create with family members picture riddles like the one in *Who Is Ben?*

CENTER WORKSHOPS

MATERIALS

- Sensory box (any box with a lid and a hole, large enough for a child's hand, cut into one side)

What Am I?

Partners Place inside the box an assortment of objects whose names begin with the letter *Aa*. You might include an apple, a toy alligator, and a plastic ant. You might also include manipulatives such as magnetic letters for *Aa*.

- Partners can use their sense of touch to identify objects whose names begin with *Aa*.
- One child can peek under the lid to confirm the object identified by the partner reaching inside the box.

Observation: Are children associating the sound the letter *Aa* stands for with the beginning sound they hear in the names of the objects that they are touching?

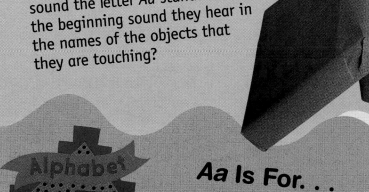

MATERIALS

- Butcher paper
- Scissors
- Pictures of *Aa* objects
- Markers
- Glue

Aa Is For. . .

Cut an apple shape from a large sheet of butcher paper. Place the paper on the floor and ask children to name the shape and letter the word *apple* begins with.

Encourage children to illustrate the apple shape with *Aa* objects.

- They can draw pictures or cut and paste photographs of objects with names that begin with *Aa*.
- Invite children to label their pictures.

Observation: What *Aa* objects or pictures do children draw or cut and paste?

DAY 6 OBJECTIVES

CHILDREN WILL:

- orally segment words (beginning sounds)
- recognize /b/
- talk about a play
- read *Birds on Stage*
- solve problems
- make a *Big Book of Riddles*
- engage in Center Workshops

MATERIALS

- *Birds on Stage*
- My Read and Write Book, pp. 9–10

GUIDED READING

To conclude each day's reading session, meet with guided reading groups. You might use Scholastic's Guided Reading Library or other books in your library.

TECHNOLOGY

 Children can interact with the **WiggleWorks Plus** selection on the computer. They can also use the **WiggleWorks Plus** Tools to innovate on the selection, to complete activities in the **WiggleWorks Plus** Write area, or to develop phonics skills on the Magnet Board.

 The song is available on the **Sounds of Phonics** audiocassette.

Share the WiggleWorks Book

DAILY PHONICS

Consonant /b/b

PHONOLOGICAL AWARENESS

Oral Segmentation: Beginning Sounds Read aloud the title of the song "Bingo." Ask children what sound they hear at the beginning of the word *Bingo*. Invite children to repeat the word as you exaggerate the beginning sound.

- Then sing the song. Invite children to sing along during a second singing.
- During later songs, have children suggest other names that begin with **/b/** to replace *Bingo*.

Bingo

There was a farmer had a dog,
And Bingo was his name-o.
B-I-N-G-O, B-I-N-G-O, B-I-N-G-O,
And Bingo was his name-o.

Build Background

ORAL LANGUAGE: PLAYS AND PERFORMANCES

Ask children if they have ever seen a performance on a stage. Encourage children to share what they remember about the performance. Include the words *curtain, lights, actors, costumes, audience,* and *scenery* in your discussion.

▶ **What do you call people who are in a play? What do they wear when they perform?**

▶ **What other kinds of performances are on stage?**

PREVIEW AND PREDICT

Show the cover of *Birds on Stage* and read the author's and illustrator's names. Encourage children to tell where they think the birds might be.

SET A PURPOSE

Have children predict what the book will be about.

Read the WiggleWorks Book

FOCUS ON RIDDLES AND RHYMES

Read the book with children, pointing to the words as you read. Encourage children to try and figure out the riddles. Have children listen for and point out the words that rhyme in each riddle.

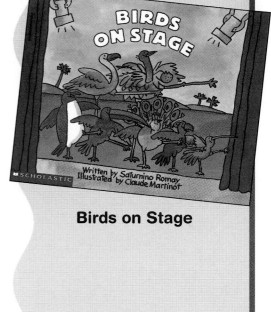

Birds on Stage

Respond to the Literature

TALK ABOUT IT

Share Personal Responses Invite children to talk about their favorite parts of the book.

► What did you like the best about reading *Birds on Stage?*

► Have you ever read a book of riddles before? What helped you solve the riddles?

► Which bird do you think is the most interesting? Why?

THINK ABOUT IT

Explore Different Solutions Review the book and talk together about the clues and answers to the riddles.

► After you hear the clues, what do you know about the bird?

► Could some of the clues describe other things?

► What else is as green as a pea? as pink as a rose? hums like a bee?

MODIFY Instruction

ESL/ELD

▲ Children acquiring English may need additional support to solve the riddles. In this case, consider using index cards. Explain the meaning of the words, and write them on the chalkboard. Then children can write the words on one side of the index cards and illustrate them on the other side. **(USE INDEX CARDS)**

Shared Writing

MAKE A *BIG* BOOK OF RIDDLES

Create a variation of *Birds on Stage,* choosing a subject such as animals. Work with children to choose several animals and to think of clues for each one.

• Write each clue on a large sheet of paper. Each clue should end with the sentence "What can it be?"

• The first time you write the sentence, leave out the question mark.

• Ask children what is missing from the end of the sentence. Encourage volunteers to add the question mark.

• Ask volunteers to write the answers to each riddle on the back of the page by writing the letters that stand for the sounds they know.

• Children can work in small groups to illustrate each page. Bind the pages together to make your own *Big Book of Riddles.*

My Read and Write Book, pp. 9–10

Repeated Reading

FOCUS ON PROBLEM-SOLVING

Reread the story with children, focusing on the specific clues that help them answer the riddles.

▶ **Which words give you clues to help you figure out the answer?**

Encourage children to predict the answer to each clue before you turn the page.

READ AND WRITE INDEPENDENTLY

Journal Place *Birds on Stage* in the Reading Center for children to enjoy on their own or in small groups. Children might enjoy writing in their Journals about their favorite bird.

 ## Comprehension Check

ACT IT OUT

Talk about how the birds in the story move and what they are doing. Encourage children to act as if they are the different birds performing on stage.

CENTER WORKSHOPS

Bird Watch

Provide each child with a book of five to ten blank pages stapled together. Explain that children will be bird watchers and keep an observation log of the birds they see and find.

- Assemble books on birds from your local library, or collect copies of nature magazines that include pictures of birds.

- Encourage children to draw pictures of the birds from the library books or to cut out pictures of birds from the magazines.

- Go on a bird-watching walk. Encourage children to draw and write in their logs about the birds they see.

Observation: What birds do children cut out pictures of or draw? How do they identify them?

MATERIALS

- Paper
- Markers
- Stapler
- Nature magazines
- Scissors

Clay Birds

Children can recreate the birds in the story or other birds. Provide children with a wide variety of art supplies and encourage them to explore different materials and techniques.

- Encourage children to describe their birds. Record what they say on a chart.

- Display children's bird creations along with the chart.

Observation: Watch how children use the clay and other materials and notice any new techniques they try. How do they describe their birds?

MATERIALS

- Colored clay
- Colored feathers
- Buttons
- *Birds on Stage*
- Chart paper

DAY 7 OBJECTIVES

CHILDREN WILL:

- listen for beginning sounds
- identify /b/b and write *Bb*
- demonstrate visual literacy
- revisit the High-Frequency Reader: *I Am*
- review high-frequency words
- engage in Center Workshops

MATERIALS

- *Apples, Alligators and also Alphabets*
- Picture Cards, R33–34
- *Problem Solving,* SourceCard 1
- High-Frequency Reader: *I Am*
- My Alphabet Book, p. 4

TECHNOLOGY

Encourage children to use the drawing and writing tools in the **WiggleWorks Plus** Write area to complete the activities in this lesson.

My Alphabet Book, p. 4

Read the SourceCard

DAILY PHONICS

Consonant /b/b

Ⓐ PHONOLOGICAL AWARENESS

Oddity Task Mix *Bb* picture cards with picture cards of words that begin with other letters. Together, say the words aloud. Ask children to identify the words that begin with **/b/.** Use the following picture cards:

bat	leaf	moon	bus
sun	bee	nut	rock

Ⓑ CONNECT SOUND-SPELLING

Introduce Consonant /b/b Page through *Apples, Alligators and also Alphabets* until you get to the *Bb* page. Point out that the letter *b* stands for /b/ as in **bird.**

- Ask children to say the sound with you.
- Say the **/b/** words on the page and have children repeat them after you.

Letter Formation

WRITE THE LETTER

Write *Bb* on the chalkboard. Point out the capital and small forms of the letter. Model how to write the letter using the rhymes provided.

- Have children write both forms of the letter in the air with their fingers. Ask children to make the letter's sound as they practice writing.

B	b
Draw a line straight down and go back to the start. *(Pull down straight, move pencil back to top.)* Then curve around and around like a sideways heart. *(Make two sideways loops.)*	Go straight down, then up halfway. *(Pull down straight, retrace halfway up.)* Circle around and back to stay. *(Circle to the right and back to the line.)*

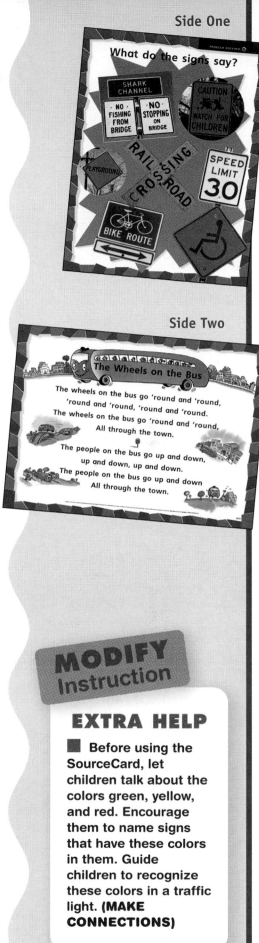

Side One

Side Two

Share the SourceCard

SIDE ONE

Read Signs Guide children to look at the photographs of the signs. Read the question, "What do the signs say?"

Encourage children to talk about the different signs in the picture. Read the signs together.

▶ **What do the signs tell you?**

▶ **Do all of the signs have words or do some only have pictures?**

Invite children to name the different shapes and colors of the signs. Talk together about how the shapes and colors help people recognize the signs.

SIDE TWO

Sing a Song Read the words to the song "The Wheels on the Bus." Emphasize the words that repeat. Then sing the song, inviting children to sing along. Encourage children to respond with hand and body movements as they sing "round and round" and "up and down."

Talk with children about why people ride in a bus.

▶ **Why might people take a bus instead of driving in a car? Why might they take a bus instead of walking?**

▶ **Have you ever been in a bus? What does it feel like when the bus is moving?**

Shared Writing

MAKE WORD CARDS

Children can make word cards for the song "The Wheels on the Bus."

• Provide a sheet of paper for each child. Point to the word *round* in the song and ask children to write *round* using the letters that stand for the sounds they know.

• Provide another sheet of paper. Ask children to write the sounds they know for the word *up* on one side and for the word *down* on the other side.

• Sing "The Wheels on the Bus" together and invite children to hold up the corresponding word card as they sing each word.

MODIFY Instruction

EXTRA HELP

■ Before using the SourceCard, let children talk about the colors green, yellow, and red. Encourage them to name signs that have these colors in them. Guide children to recognize these colors in a traffic light. **(MAKE CONNECTIONS)**

I Am

Instruction

ESL/ELD

▲ Use sticky notes to cover the last word in each sentence. Model how to use the picture clues to figure out the missing word. For example, if the whole sentence is *I am hungry,* you should point to yourself and a picture of food. **(PANTOMIME)**

Revisit High-Frequency Reader

REREAD THE BOOK
Invite children to join you as you read *I Am* again. On the first page, have children read the two words they have already learned (*I* and *am*). Review these words.

DECODING STRATEGIES
As you go through the book, point to each word, the initial letter and other sound-spellings children have learned, and the picture clue, pausing long enough for children to read before you do. Model blending words, as necessary. For example, point out the **/b/** in *building* and help children read the word.

> **Think Aloud** *At the beginning of the word I see the letter* **b.** *I know that* **b** *stands for /b/. In the picture I see a child building. The word* **building** *begins with /b/. This word is* **building.** *That makes sense in the sentence.*

CONCEPTS OF PRINT: TRACKING
Display the sentence strips for the High-Frequency Reader. Have children read aloud with you as you track the print with a finger. Then have volunteers track the words while the group reads along.

ORAL LANGUAGE: ACTION WORDS
Talk about the activity that the child is doing on each page of the story. Invite children to tell which of these activities they have done and to name other activities they enjoy.

READ FOR FLUENCY
Give each child their own copy of *I Am.* Have children read the book with a partner. Partners can take turns acting out the activity the child is doing on each page.

READ AND WRITE INDEPENDENTLY
Journal Place copies of *I Am* in the Reading Center. Let children read the book on their own or in small groups. Encourage children to have a conversation about activities they enjoy. Then children can write in their Journals about these activities.

HOME/SCHOOL CONNECTION
Children can take home their High-Frequency Reader and work with family members on a new book about the activities that they do together.

CENTER WORKSHOPS

Drawing Signs

Place copies of *What Am I?* and the SourceCard in the Art Center. Invite children to draw signs that they see on the SourceCard or those that they know from their own experiences, such as stop signs, store signs, and road signs.

• Encourage children to refer to the cutout shapes in the book in order to draw signs with different shapes. They can use colored construction paper to create signs in different colors. Invite children to cut out their signs and post them on a bulletin board.

Observation: Which signs do children make? How do they go about choosing the shapes?

MATERIALS

• Colored construction paper
• Markers, crayons
• Scissors
• *What Am I?*
• *Problem Solving,* SourceCard 1

MATERIALS

• Blocks
• Small toy cars, buses, and other vehicles
• Markers or crayons
• Index cards or paper

Our Town

Let children use blocks to build a pretend town. Guide them to construct buildings, roads and bridges. Help them make signs to designate features and buildings.

Children can use toy vehicles to take pretend "trips" through the town and describe what they see along the way.

You might suggest that children use blocks to create maze-like roadways and tunnels. Talk about how to make the mazes easier or more difficult.

Observation: How do children use blocks to create mazes and tunnels?

DAY 8 OBJECTIVES

CHILDREN WILL:

- orally blend onsets and rimes
- review consonant /b/b
- read and respond to *Where's My Teddy?*
- recognize and use size words
- relate the story to personal experience
- compare and contrast stories
- write lost and found signs
- engage in Center Workshops

MATERIALS

- *Where's My Teddy?*

Share the Read Aloud

DAILY PHONICS

Consonant /b/b

Ⓐ PHONOLOGICAL AWARENESS

Oral Blending Say the following word parts. Ask children to blend them to make a word. Provide corrective feedback and modeling when necessary.

/b/ . . . all	/b/ . . . and	/b/ . . . at
/b/ . . . ox	/b/ . . . ug	/b/ . . . ack

Ⓑ CONNECT SOUND-SPELLING

Bear's Book Draw the outline of a large book on chart paper. Write the words *Bear's Book* on the left-hand page. Circle the letter **B** and say the words aloud. Remind children that the letter **B** stands for **/b/**. Invite children to suggest words that begin with **/b/**. Write each word and have volunteers circle the letter **b**. Then read "Bear's Book" together.

Build Background

ORAL LANGUAGE: SIZE WORDS

Invite children to recall some words in *The Three Bears* that describe the size of the bears and the items in their home. Then ask children to think of other words that mean *little* or *big*. Make a "Big" and "Little" word web.

PREVIEW AND PREDICT

Examine the cover of the book with children. Read the title and the author's and illustrator's names. Encourage children to speculate why the bear on the cover might have a teddy.

▶ **Why do you think the bear is running?**

SET A PURPOSE

Invite children to listen to the story to find out why the bear is running through the woods with a teddy.

Share the Read Aloud

TALK ABOUT CHARACTER'S FEELINGS

Read the story, pausing to let children respond. Encourage them to talk about how Eddie might be feeling as he seeks and finds Freddie.

Respond to the Literature

TALK ABOUT IT

Share Personal Responses Invite children to share their personal responses to the story and to talk about what they liked best.

▶ **What did you like best about the book?**

▶ **What parts of the story could be real?**

▶ **What parts remind you of other stories?**

▶ **What might have happened if the boy had taken the giant teddy bear home?**

THINK ABOUT IT

Compare/Contrast Stories The story is told from Eddie's point of view. Ask children to think about the story the big bear would tell.

▶ **What would be different?**

▶ **What would be the same?**

Then make a chart together comparing *The Three Bears* and *Where's My Teddy?* List the characters and the places where each story takes place.

Where's My Teddy?

MODIFY Instruction

EXTRA HELP

■ Provide additional support by keeping a copy of *The Three Bears* on display during the Build Background activity. As you read the story, pause frequently and allow ample time for children to begin making connections between *The Three Bears* and *Where's My Teddy?* Use guided questions to help children share their points of view when comparing the two stories. **(COMPARE AND CONTRAST)**

OBSERVATION

How are children doing? Are they:

- suggesting words that compare sizes?
- including important information in their lost-and-found posters?
- acting out story events accurately?

MODIFY Instruction

ESL/ELD

▲ Encourage children acquiring English to share words in their native language that compare sizes. List these on chart paper next to the English equivalents. Model pronunciation for children. (COMPARE/CONTRAST)

Shared Writing

MAKE A LOST-AND-FOUND POSTER

Explain to children that sometimes people make and post signs when they lose something. That way, other people might help them find what they lost. Talk about the kind of information you would put on such a sign so that others would know just what you were looking for. Ideas might include:

- name of lost object
- words to tell what it looks like
- place where it was lost
- picture of the object
- owner's name
- telephone or classroom number

Children can make signs for items they pretend to have lost. Suggest that they create stories about the lost items. Children can also make signs for any personal items they might have lost and post them around school.

Repeated Reading

COMPARE SIZES

Reread the story together, asking children to look and listen for words and pictures that describe sizes. Make a list of the size words children find. Invite children to make size comparisons about the things they see in the illustrations.

▶ **How would you describe Eddie's teddy?**

▶ **What words describe the bear's teddy?**

READ AND WRITE INDEPENDENTLY

Journal Place *Where's My Teddy?* in the Reading Center so that children can read it on their own or in small groups. Children can write in their Journals about one of the teddies in the story, or about a teddy or stuffed animal of their own.

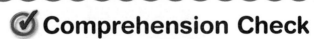

✅ Comprehension Check

ACT IT OUT

Reread the story. Then invite children to act it out. Children can work in teams, taking turns being the bear or Eddie.

CENTER WORKSHOPS

MATERIALS

- Construction paper
- Crayons or markers
- Blocks
- Information books about bears
- Sticky notes
- *Where's My Teddy?*

Bears' Beds

Share and discuss the picture of the bear in his bed at the end of *Where's My Teddy?* Encourage children to imagine and illustrate or build what a bear's home might look like. After they have completed their bear homes, invite children to look through the books for pictures of bears in their natural settings. They can use sticky notes to mark any pages that show bears' homes or bears' beds. Then, gather together to look at and talk about the children's illustrations, block homes, and the reference book pictures.

Observation: Notice what elements children incorporate into their bear habitats.

Plenty of Prints

Children can make and sort different kinds of prints. Encourage children to use the clay to make their own fingerprints, toe prints, hand prints, footprints, and knuckle prints.

Children can place their prints on a table. The other children can try to guess what part of the body made each print.

Observation: Watch how children use the clues in each print to guess how it was made.

MATERIALS

- Clay
- Rolling pin
- Forks
- Bottle caps
- *Where's My Teddy?*

DAY 9 OBJECTIVES

CHILDREN WILL:

- orally segment words
- read a rhyme
- review /b/b
- connect speaking and writing
- review high-frequency words
- read My Book: *Hair*
- engage in Center Workshops

MATERIALS

- *Big Book of Rhymes and Rhythms,* p. 7
- *Sentence Strips for "Baa, Baa, Black Sheep"*
- *Apples, Alligators and also Alphabets*
- *Where's My Teddy?*
- ABC Card for *Bb*
- *My Read and Write Book,* p. 11

My Read and Write Book, p. 11

For additional practice see *Scholastic Phonics K,* pp. 15–18. Also see Sound and Letter Book: *What Can It Be?*

Sounds and Letters

DAILY PHONICS

And Read My Book

Consonant /b/b

Ⓐ PHONOLOGICAL AWARENESS

Oral Segmentation: Beginning Sounds
Read aloud "Baa, Baa, Black Sheep," from the *Big Book of Rhymes and Rhythms.* Ask children what sound they hear at the beginning of the words *Baa, bags,* and *boy.* Invite them to repeat the words with you as you emphasize the beginning sound. Then ask children to think of other words that begin with **/b/.**

Big Book of Rhymes and Rhythms, p. 7

Ⓑ CONCEPTS OF PRINT

Develop Print Awareness Put the *Big Book of Rhymes and Rhythms,* the Sentence Strips for "Baa, Baa, Black Sheep," and a pocket chart in the Reading Center.

- Read the rhyme, asking children to tap their hands on a table in time with the rhythm.

- Reread the rhyme together. Ask volunteers to place the Sentence Strip that shows each line in the pocket chart as it is read.

- Then invite children to point to and read the words that begin with *Bb.*

Baa, baa, black sheep,
Have you any wool?
Yes sir! Yes sir!
Three bags full.

MODIFY
Instruction

EXTRA HELP

■ Help children visualize the letter *Bb* in words on your classroom list by chunking the words in syllables. Highlight the syllables with the letter *Bb.* Read the syllable, pointing out the letter *Bb*, and ask children to repeat it after you. Then read the whole word and have children do the same. **[STEP-BY-STEP]**

Ⓒ CONNECT SOUND-SPELLING

Alphabetic Principle Remind children that the letter *b* stands for **/b/** as in *ball.* Ask children to open the ABC book *Apples, Alligators and also Alphabets* to the **Bb** page and identify as many pictures as they can whose names begin with **/b/.** For example: *boots, bathtub, brush, bow, buttons.*

ABC Book Explain to children that they are going to make a new page for their ABC book. Have children suggest animals, objects, and people whose names begin with **/b/.** Invite children to work together to create the *Bb* page for their ABC Books.

Then display the ABC Card for *Bb* (if available) and have children say the name of the letter and the picture.

Environmental Print Children may enjoy labeling classroom areas or items whose names begin with *Bb*, such as *bulletin boards, books, blocks,* and *bathroom.* Make a list. Encourage children to make labels using the name and a drawing of the item or place. Help children place their labels throughout the classroom.

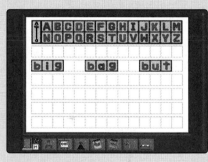

TECHNOLOGY

Children can write the words *big, bag,* and *but* horizontally on the **WiggleWorks Plus** Magnet Board. Encourage children to place a *B* above each vowel and to add another letter beneath it to complete a word vertically. Offer clues such as: *just a little _____; something used to hit a baseball; it means "insect."*

Ⓓ VOCABULARY: HIGH-FREQUENCY WORDS

Write the incomplete sentence *I am* _____ on the chalkboard. Then do the following:

• Review each high-frequency word in the sentence. If necessary, review the read-spell-write routine for each word.

• Place the word **big** in the blank space. Invite a volunteer to read the new sentence.

• Then ask children to suggest other words to complete the sentence. Invite volunteers to read each new sentence aloud.

The rhyme from the *Big Book of Rhythms and Rhymes* is available on the **Sounds of Phonics** audiocassette.

Hair

MODIFY Instruction

ESL/ELD

▲ Read the My Book to small groups of children. As you read, point to the illustrations that describe different types of hair. Then ask volunteers to point to the illustration that looks like their own hair and describe it. Provide them with sentence starters: *My hair is _____.* **(MAKE CONNECTIONS)**

Read My Book

INTRODUCE THE BOOK

Let the children know that they are going to get their own book that they can read on their own and take home.

▶ **What words can you use to describe hair?**

PREVIEW AND PREDICT

Pass out copies of *Hair*. Read the author's and illustrator's names. Ask children about the illustration on the cover.

▶ **What is the girl looking at? What might this book be about?**

READ TOGETHER

Read the My Book with children, tracking the print as you read. Guide children to read along in their copies and to notice the types of hair pictured in the illustrations. When children finish reading, invite them to think of questions that can be answered by the word *hair*, such as, "What is on your head?" or "What is under your hat?"

PHONICS

Ask children to say the word **be** aloud.

▶ **What letter stands for the sound you hear at the beginning of the word?**

READ AND WRITE INDEPENDENTLY

Journal Encourage children to read *Hair* on their own or in small groups. Invite children to color the illustrations.

HOME/SCHOOL CONNECTIONS

Children can take home their My Book to share with family members and friends. Suggest that children work with family members to draw and think of words to describe the family members' hair.

CENTER WORKSHOPS

Bb Finger Paint Fun

Children can practice writing the letter *Bb* in finger paint. Provide the ABC Cards for children to use as a guide. Encourage children to explore using finger paint.

- Ask children about the colors they're using and the shapes and kinds of lines they are making.

Observation: Are children writing uppercase and lowercase *Bb*'s? Do they recognize the connection between the letter *Bb* and the /b/ sound?

MATERIALS

- *Bb* ABC Cards
- Paper
- Blue, brown, and black finger paint

Our Beautiful Bears

Give each child colored clay to mold into the shape of a bear. Children can etch a face onto their bears if they wish. When the bears are completed, children can label them, such as "Jenny's brown bear" and display them on a shelf with the heading "Our Beautiful Bears."

- Children can also mold clay snakes into big *Bb*'s, medium-sized *Bb*'s, and little *Bb*'s.

Observation: Notice if children are talking about words that begin with the letter *Bb*.

MATERIALS

- Colored clay (brown, black, and blue)
- Rolling pins
- Etching tools
- Plastic knives
- Pictures or models of bears on display

Put It All Together

DAY 10 OBJECTIVES

CHILDREN WILL:

- follow oral directions
- listen to and identify clues
- compare and contrast the books they've shared
- participate in writing a group chart
- create alliterative sentences
- maintain /a/a, /b/b
- make a clay diorama

MATERIALS

- *What Am I?*
- *Birds On Stage*
- *Where's My Teddy?*
- *The Three Bears*

TECHNOLOGY

 Encourage children to use the drawing and writing tools in the **WiggleWorks Plus** Write area to complete the project and activities.

Sum It Up

USING CLUES TO PREDICT

Ask children about the many ways they have used story clues to predict events in the stories they have read.

▶ **What were the different clues?**

▶ **How did the clues help?**

▶ **Did the clues help you guess correctly?**

ORAL LANGUAGE: CLUE WORDS

Play "Treasure Hunt" with children. When the treasure is found, encourage children to talk about how they used the clues during the hunt.

▶ **How did the clues help you find the treasure?**

Treasure Hunt

1. In advance, hide a treasure, such as a special snack, a new book for the Reading Center, or a new set of coloring materials.

2. Prepare a series of clues that will act as an oral treasure map to lead children to the treasure.

3. Plant clues at various locations and lead children from clue to clue and finally to the treasure.

COMPARE AND CONTRAST CHART

Language Experience Chart

Display the four books children have read during the previous sessions. Invite children to have a conversation in which they share their feelings about the books. Make a language chart with the heading "Clues We Use." Write the names of the books across the top of the chart.

Invite children to discuss the types of clues used in each book. List the clues under the book title.

Encourage children to add pictures to the chart. As children draw their pictures, ask them to tell how they used the clues in the story.

MODIFY Instruction

GIFTED & TALENTED

✳ Help children notice that story clues contain important information by asking them to summarize the stories based on these clues. After you and the children complete the chart, invite volunteers to tell each story, referring to clues from the chart. Guide children to notice that the clues help them remember what the story is about. **(SUMMARIZE)**

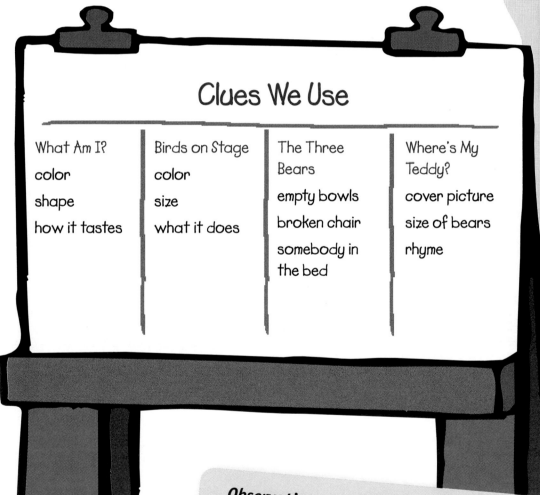

Clues We Use

What Am I?	Birds on Stage	The Three Bears	Where's My Teddy?
color	color	empty bowls	cover picture
shape	size	broken chair	size of bears
how it tastes	what it does	somebody in the bed	rhyme

Observation

How are children doing? Are they:
- creating and using clues to make predictions?
- asking questions to explore the clues being used?
- making connections between stories they have read?

DAILY PHONICS

Maintenance

Ⓐ PHONOLOGICAL AWARENESS

Silly Sentences Read the following alliterative sentence aloud and have children repeat it with you. Then ask children to count the number of times they hear /b/ and name the **Bb** words.

Big beautiful bears and a bunch of bugs bounce on boxes.

Encourage children to make up their own silly sentences using words that begin with /b/. Children may enjoy illustrating their sentences.

Ⓑ PHONICS MAINTENANCE

Picture Sound Match Review **Aa** and **Bb** with children by displaying picture cards that show objects whose names begin with /a/ or /b/. Some additional pictures that you can add to your picture cards include: *ax, ant, apple, alligator, banana, ball, box, boy, bear, bag.*

• Divide the class into two groups and assign each group a sound. One can be the /a/ group and the other can be the /b/ group. Distribute picture cards and challenge children to find those that begin with their sound.

• Give each child a picture card. Hold up a letter card for **Aa** and ask the children who have a picture card that begins with /a/ to stand up. Then have volunteers show their picture card and say the /a/ word for the class. Repeat this activity for words that begin with /b/.

WEEKS 1 AND 2
PROJECT

Tell a Story With Clay

During the past two weeks, children have explored a variety of ways to identify and solve problems. For the project, children can select a story, create characters and scenery, and dramatize literature. In Weeks 5 and 6, children will have a celebration, inviting family members and friends to view the many dioramas and other things they have created. Keep children's creations in a safe place so they can be displayed at the celebration.

Let children know that they can use clay to retell one of the stories they have read. Guide children to work together to select one of the stories. Talk with children about their story preferences, encouraging them to explain why they like a particular story.

- When the story is selected, invite children to revisit it through another reading, the audiocassette, or their own retellings. Post chart paper and encourage children to make a list of the characters and objects in the story. Label the chart and post it for future reference.

- Encourage children to talk together to decide who will be responsible for making each character and object they wish to include.

- Children can work together or on their own to create the story characters and other objects in the claymator's studio.

- When the creation is finished, display it where children and visiting family members can view it.

Portfolio Photographs provide a permanent reminder of the entire learning process. Keeping an ongoing photo album enables children to recall their work and allows family members to share in their child's school experience. This kind of documentation can be used in a variety of ways throughout the school year. It also provides a way to monitor children's reactions to certain activities.

MATERIALS

- Book or audiocassette of the selected story
- Chart paper
- Markers
- Clay

BENCHMARKS

Monitor children's progress. Are they

- listening for clues?
- beginning to use clues to solve problems?

WEEKS
3 AND 4

Kindergarten Goals
for Weeks 3 and 4

Oral Language/ Vocabulary

- participating in rhymes, songs, conversations, and discussions
- participating in choral reading
- exploring color words, weather words, problem solving words
- exploring story vocabulary

Reading

- building alphabetic knowledge
- participating actively in shared reading
- engaging in emergent reading
- exploring concepts of print
- participating with patterned text
- retelling order of events in stories
- making predictions
- distinguishing fantasy from reality
- reading high-frequency words

Writing

- playing with alliteration
- labeling with color words
- writing letters: *Cc, Dd*
- writing describing words
- creating questions
- writing a recipe
- writing a cumulative story
- engaging in shared writing
- writing independently in Journals
- writing a language-experience chart

Listening/Speaking/ Viewing

- listening responsively to texts read aloud
- identifying rhyme
- developing phonological awareness
- listening to stories on tape
- retelling a story in their own words
- presenting dramatic interpretations of stories
- singing songs
- engaging in conversations
- relating personal experiences to literature
- demonstrating visual literacy

Daily Phonics: *Cc* and *Dd*

- reciting classic poems, songs, and nursery rhymes
- naming and recognizing the letters
- recognizing sound/letter relationships
- generating words that begin with /k/, /d/
- decoding words using beginning sounds

Center Workshops and Project

- acquiring world knowledge through cross-curricular activities
- creating a storyboard

WEEKS 3 AND 4 RESOURCES

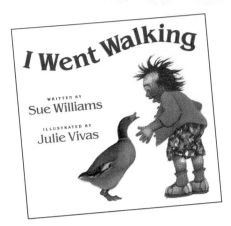

Big Book

Meet the Author
Sue Williams lives on a farm in Australia. She wrote *I Went Walking* for her nieces and nephews.

Meet the Illustrator
Julie Vivas is an Australian illustrator who uses watercolor to create her illustrations.

Available as audiocassette

Big Book of Rhymes and Rhythms

For teaching phonological awareness, the alphabet, and concepts of print.

- "Little Boy Blue"
- "Hickory, Dickory, Dock"

Available as audiocassette

Read Aloud

Meet the Author/ Illustrator
Esphyr Slobodkina was born in Siberia, Russia, in 1909. She believed in writing children's books that would challenge the child's mind and thinking.

Read Aloud

Meet the Author
The culture of the Southwest has always interested Jan Romero Stevens. *Carlos and the Squash Plant* is her first book for children.

Meet the Illustrator
Jeanne Arnold studied the works of Diego Rivera and the Taos painters to make the illustrations in this story realistic and authentic.

ABC Book

Meet the Authors/ Illustrators
Odette Johnson creates clay animation for television at Quack Quack animation in Toronto, Canada. She likes to work with clay and enjoys making three-dimensional, brightly colored sculptures.

Side One

Side Two

SourceCard
- How many ways are there to get from the school to the library?
- When would you wear these shoes?

High-Frequency Reader

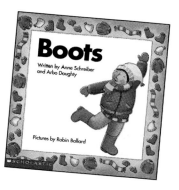

Boots
Written by Anne Schreiber and Arbo Doughty
Pictures by Robin Ballard

My Read and Write Book

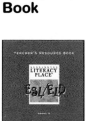

My Alphabet Book

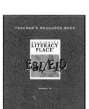

ESL/ELD Teaching Guide

My Books

To take home to share.

GETTING READY
by Cass Hollander
Illustrated by Pamela Bonnell

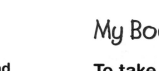

TIME TO GET UP!
by Cass Hollander
Illustrated by Vincent Andriani

Introducing the Mentor

Becky Wible works at a studio in New Jersey with a team of animators. They work together to solve problems, sharing ideas and trying different solutions.

DAYS AT A GLANCE

WEEKS 3 AND 4

	Daily Phonics	Literature	Shared Writing	Workshops and Projects
DAY 1	Phonological Awareness: Oral Segmentation: Beginning Sounds Review /a/a, /b/b	*Apples, Alligators and also Alphabets* by Odette and Bruce Johnson ABC BOOK	Compose Alliterative Sentences	Alphabet: Raining Animals Art: Clay *Cc's* and *Dd's*
DAY 2	**Consonant /k/c** Phonological Awareness: Oral Segmentation: Beginning Sounds	*I Went Walking* by Sue Williams illustrated by Julie Vivas BIG BOOK·LITTLE BOOK	Label with Color Words	Science: Mixing Colors Art: Flying Colors
DAY 3	**Consonant /k/c** Phonological Awareness: Oral Blending Introduce Sound-Spelling	*I Went Walking* by Sue Williams BIG BOOK·LITTLE BOOK **High-Frequency Reader:** *I Can See*	Concepts of Print: Questions and Periods Write *Cc* Write Class Book	Games: Do You Have a Clue? Art: Color Collages
DAY 4	**Consonant /k/c** Phonological Awareness: Oddity Task: Beginning Sound Review Sound-Spelling	*Caps for Sale* by Esphyr Slobodkina READ ALOUD	Write Describing Words	Art: The Peddler's Caps Dramatic Play: Monkey See, Monkey Do!
DAY 5	**Consonant /k/c** Phonological Awareness: Auditory Discrimination Maintain Sound-Spelling	**"Little Boy Blue"** a poem *Apples, Alligators and also Alphabets* **My Book:** *Getting Ready*	Concepts of Print: Words that Begin with *Cc* High-Frequency Words: *a, you, can*	Cooking: A Case of Carrots! Dramatic Play: Are You Ready?

	Daily Phonics	Literature	Shared Writing	Workshops and Projects
DAY 6	Consonant /d/d Phonological Awareness: Rhyme	*Boots* by Anne Schreiber and Arbo Doughty	Write a Cumulative Story	Art: Self Portrait Writing: Writing Sentences
DAY 7	Consonant /d/d Phonological Awareness: Alliteration Introduce Sound-Spelling	SourceCard Ways to Get There Shoes **High-Frequency Reader:** *I Can See*	Write Place Names Write *Dd*	Art: Drawing a Town Math: If the Shoe Fits
DAY 8	Consonant /d/d Phonological Awareness: Oral Blending Review Sound-Spelling	*Carlos and the Squash Plant* by Jan Romero Stevens illustrated by Jeanne Arnold READ ALOUD	Write a Recipe	Science: Explore Dirt Science: Wash and Dry
DAY 9	Consonant /d/d Phonological Awareness: Rhyme Maintain Sound-Spelling	"Hickory, Dickory, Dock" a song *I Went Walking* **My Book:** *Time to Get Up*	Concepts of Print: Connect Speaking and Writing	Music & Movement: Do a *Dd* Dance Alphabet: In Search of *Dd*'s
DAY 10	Phonological Awareness: Rhyme Phonics Maintenance	**Review Books from Weeks 3 and 4**	Make a Compare and Contrast Language Chart	Project: Create a Storyboard

Share the ABC Book

DAILY PHONICS

Warm-Up: Wordplay

Ⓐ PHONOLOGICAL AWARENESS

Abby Likes . . . Play the game "Abby likes . . . ." Explain that Abby only likes things that begin with /a/. Ask children to identify which of these things Abby likes: *apples, bugs, carrots, ants, alligators, dogs*. Repeat with "Billy likes . . . " and these words: *balls, trucks, beans, bats, soda, berries*.

Ⓑ PHONICS MAINTENANCE

Review Vowel /a/a, Consonant /b/b Open *Apples, Alligators and also Alphabets* to the pages for *a* and *b*. Have children name the letters and say the sound each one stands for. Ask which objects on the pages Abby and Billy might like.

Build Background

ORAL LANGUAGE: MAKING ART

Explain that the artists created the pictures in *Apples, Alligators and also Alphabets* using clay. Ask children to think about the different kinds of artwork they have seen.

▶ **What did the artists use to make their artwork?**

▶ **What have you made with clay?**

▶ **What other art materials have you used?**

Organize children's responses in a word web.

PREVIEW AND PREDICT

Show the cover of the ABC book and read aloud the title, tracking the print. Point to the illustration and ask:

▶ **What do you remember about this book?**

▶ **How can you tell that this is an ABC book?**

▶ **Why do you think this book begins with pictures of things that begin with the letter A?**

clay · crayons · Art · paint · wood · metal · yarn

Read the ABC Book

ALPHABETIC KNOWLEDGE: Cc AND Dd

Read aloud the ABC book. As you read, invite volunteers to point to and name the objects on each page. When you get to the *Cc* and *Dd* pages, introduce the letters. Encourage children to find additional objects in the artwork that begin with **/k/** and **/d/**. For every object they find, say the word again and point to the beginning letter.

Odette and Bruce Johnson

Apples, Alligators and also Alphabets

Respond to the Literature

TALK ABOUT IT

Share Personal Responses Guide children to have conversations with one another about the book, using the following questions:

▶ **Which pictures do you find funny?**

▶ **Did the author/illustrators include any objects in the artwork that you did not expect to see?**

▶ **What new words did you hear?**

THINK ABOUT IT

Focus on Cc and Dd Review with children the letters they have learned—**/a/a, /b/b.** Then tell children that they will be focusing on the letters *Cc* and *Dd*. Turn to the *Cc* page in the ABC book. Invite children to name the objects in the picture.

▶ **What sound do you hear at the beginning of each word?**

▶ **What other words do you know that begin with this sound?**

Write some of the words children suggest on the board. Have them point to the beginning letter. Repeat the same procedure for the *Dd* page. Invite children to illustrate the words.

EXTRA HELP

■ Have children sit in a circle and play the alphabet name game using the letters *A*, *B*, *C*, and *D*. Model an example using the letter *A*.

A—My name is Alice and I like apples.

Encourage children to point to a picture of something they like for each letter in the ABC book and then complete the sentence with the name of the picture. **(MODEL)**

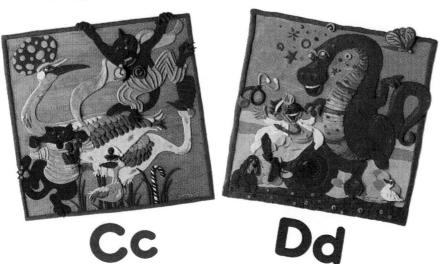

Cc   Dd

MODIFY
Instruction

ESL/ELD

▲ Help children brainstorm a list of words for each sound before they compose their alliterative sentences. Make sure they understand the meaning of the words they will be using. **(BRAINSTORM)**

PROFESSIONAL DEVELOPMENT

GAY SU PINNELL

Interactive Writing

Children need to engage in independent, guided, shared, and interactive writing every week. During interactive writing, teachers and students write messages and stories together using a "shared pen" technique. The teacher models the writing process, yet children participate by writing words or specific letters in words. This helps to increase spelling knowledge and apply phonics skills in writing contexts.

Shared Writing

PLAY WITH ALLITERATION

Review with children the sounds for the letters *Aa, Bb, Cc,* and *Dd*. Talk about words that begin with these sounds.

- Divide children into groups. Ask them to work together to compose sentences in which many of the words begin with the sound for one of these letters. Provide an example such as, "Can a cat cut a carrot?"

- Tell children that their sentences can be silly and do not need to make sense. As children share their sentences, write them on the board or chart paper. Children can write the letters that stand for the sounds they know.

▶ **With which letter do most of the words begin?**

Invite volunteers to underline the target letter in each word. Invite groups to illustrate their sentences.

Repeated Reading

TELL PICTURE STORIES

Reread the ABC book with children. Invite children to tell in their own words what is happening in the pictures on each page.

▶ **Who is on this page?**

▶ **What are they doing?**

▶ **How do they seem to be feeling?**

Encourage children to make up stories for their favorite pages.

READ AND WRITE INDEPENDENTLY

Journal Place several copies of *Apples, Alligators and also Alphabets* in the Reading Center for children to read independently or with a partner. Have children draw and label something whose name begins with the same letter as their name.

☑ Comprehension Check

ACT IT OUT

As you reread the book, children can make the shapes of the letters on each page using their hands or bodies, or by writing in sand placed in small pans.

CENTER WORKSHOPS

MATERIALS

- **Apples, Alligators and also Alphabets**
- **Pictures of cats, dogs, and other animals**
- **Paper**
- **Yarn, felt scraps, buttons, crayons**
- **Other collage materials**

Raining Animals

Children may enjoy making a mural of the animals in *Apples, Alligators and also Alphabets*—alligators, baboons, cats, dinosaurs, and so on. Children can flip through the book and decide which animal they'd like to create and then draw and label it on a mural.

Display the mural on a bulletin board labeled "It's Raining Animals!"

Observation: What animals do children choose to add to the mural?

CAT

DOG

Clay *Cc*'s and *Dd*'s

Children can manipulate clay snakes to form the letters *Cc* and *Dd*. Provide ABC Cards as models. Ask children how they can change an uppercase *C* to an uppercase *D*. How can a lowercase *c* be changed to a lowercase *d*?

Label children's creations "Clay *Cc*'s" and "Doughy *Dd*'s."

Take instant photographs of children's letter creations.

Observation: How are children demonstrating knowledge of the shapes of *Cc* and *Dd*?

MATERIALS

- **Clay**
- **Rolling pins**
- **Alphabet Cards for *Cc* and *Dd***

DAY 2 OBJECTIVES

CHILDREN WILL:

- orally segment words (beginning sounds)
- recognize consonant /k/c
- identify colors
- read and respond to *I Went Walking*
- use picture clues to make predictions
- chime in on patterned text
- engage in Center Workshops

MATERIALS

- *I Went Walking*
- **My Read and Write Book,** pp. 12–13

The Big Book is available on audiocassette in the Literacy Place Listening Center. The song is available on the **Sounds of Phonics** audiocassette.

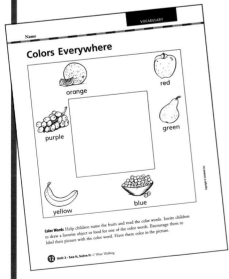

My Read and Write Book, p. 12

Share the Big Book

DAILY PHONICS

Consonant /k/c

PHONOLOGICAL AWARENESS

Oral Segmentation: Beginning Sounds Read aloud the title "She'll Be Coming Round the Mountain." Ask children what sound they hear at the beginning of *Coming*.

- Invite children to repeat the word *coming*, exaggerating the beginning sound: *c-c-coming*.
- Then sing the song. Invite children to sing along. Have children clap each time they hear a word that begins with **/k/**.

She'll Be Coming Round the Mountain

She'll be coming round
the mountain when she comes,
She'll be coming round
the mountain when she comes,
She'll be coming round the mountain,
She'll be coming round the mountain
She'll be coming round the mountain
when she comes.

Build Background

ORAL LANGUAGE: COLORS

Show children a variety of objects, each a different color. Ask children to name each color. As each color is named, write it in a word web using that color marker.

You might invite children to play a quick game of I Spy using color words for clues to identify classroom objects.

PREVIEW AND PREDICT

Display *I Went Walking*. Read the title and the names of the author and illustrator, tracking the print.

▶ Who do you think went walking?

▶ What do you think the child saw on the walk?

Read the Big Book

MAKE PREDICTIONS

Read aloud the story, tracking the print with your finger to model left-to-right progression. After the first episode, invite children to predict what animal the child will see next.

- Pause before turning the page. Point to the part of the animal in the picture that reveals what the child will see next.

- Give children enough time to look carefully at the picture clue to make predictions.

Encourage children to notice other story details in the illustrations such as where the animal is and what the child is doing.

I Went Walking

Respond to the Literature

TALK ABOUT IT

Share Personal Responses Invite children to share their reactions to the story.

▶ **What are some of the places that you like to go for a walk?**

▶ **What kinds of things do you see on your walk?**

▶ **Have you ever met any of the animals that are in this story?**

▶ **Where might you meet some of them?**

▶ **Where do you think the child in the story lives?**

THINK ABOUT IT

Make an Animal Color Chart Make a chart with a column for each color named in *I Went Walking*. Write each color word with its corresponding marker. With children, look through *I Went Walking*. Write each animal's name under the correct color. Invite children to draw the animal in the chart. Reread your animal color chart, pointing to each word. Encourage children to suggest other animals to add to each color column.

Animal Color Chart		
Black	**Brown**	**Red**
Cat	Horse	Cow
Dog	Bear	Fox

MODIFY Instruction

GIFTED & TALENTED

✳ Invite children to retell the story using picture clues. Then encourage them to tell the story again and again, adding more details with each telling. They might, for example, include the color words with the animal names, then describe the girl's reaction to each animal, and finally, comment on how the girl removes different pieces of clothing as her walk continues. **(SPIRALING)**

OBSERVATION

How are children doing? Are they:

- using picture clues to predict the story events?
- recognizing the repetitive structure of the story?
- recognizing color words?

Keep the answers to these questions in mind as you plan Day 3, Revisit the Big Book.

MODIFY Instruction

ESL/ELD

▲ Help children say descriptive sentences using color words like *It's a black cat.* Have them draw one of the animals and label it with a color and name. Children can hold up their drawings and ask: *What is this?* Have their classmates answer.
(MULTISENSORY TECHNIQUES)

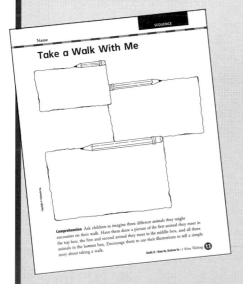

My Read and Write Book, p. 13

Shared Writing

LABEL WITH COLOR WORDS

Review with children the different color words in *I Went Walking* and those they listed on the word web.

- Then invite each child to choose one color at a time and draw pictures of items that are that color.
- Help children label their pictures with the color words.
- Display the pictures, grouping them together by color.

Repeated Reading

CHIME IN ON PATTERNED TEXT

Show children the cover of the Big Book and guide them to reread the title with you. As you reread the book, invite children to notice the text pattern.

- Encourage children to chime in on the repeated text: *I went walking. What did you see?*
- Explain how they can use pictures to supply the new animal name and color word on each page.
- Point to each word as you read together.

READ AND WRITE INDEPENDENTLY

Journal Place copies of *I Went Walking* in your Reading Center so that children can enjoy revisiting the story by themselves or with a friend.

- Encourage children to have conversations with others about the book.
- Invite children to use their Journals to draw or write about their favorite animal from the book. Encourage them to use the book to help them label their animal.

☑ Comprehension Check

ACT IT OUT

Encourage children to act out *I Went Walking.* You can narrate the story by asking, "What do you see?" Give each child a turn to play the part of the girl or an animal.

CENTER WORKSHOPS

Mixing Colors!

Working with an adult, children can gently place small drops of food coloring in containers of warm water that have been mixed with a small amount of corn starch.

Ask children how the water moves. What happens when certain colors mix? What will happen next? Children may want to try it several times.

Children can also experiment mixing paints of different color.

Observation: What observations do children make as they mix the colors?

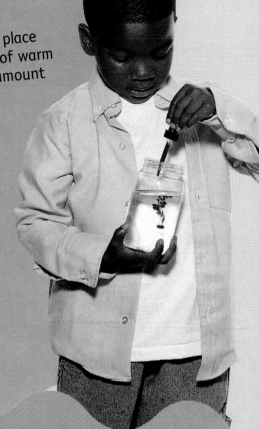

MATERIALS

- Food coloring
- Corn starch
- Warm water
- Gallon-sized plastic tubs
- Paints

Flying Colors!

Invite children to make kites using their choice of colored construction paper. Children can cut out kites modeled from pictures they see. Show them how to add string and scraps of cloth for the tail.

Children may also want to decorate their kites in a patchwork design using scraps of wrapping paper.

Observation: Notice how children create their kites.

MATERIALS

- Construction paper
- Pictures of kites
- Wrapping paper
- String
- Scraps of cloth
- Scissors
- Tape

DAY 3 OBJECTIVES

CHILDREN WILL:

- orally blend words
- identify /k/c and write *Cc*
- reread *I Went Walking*
- recognize sequence
- explore concepts of print: end punctuation
- identify the high-frequency words: *can, a*
- read High-Frequency Reader: *I Can See*
- engage in Center Workshops

MATERIALS

- *I Went Walking*
- *Apples, Alligators and also Alphabets*
- High-Frequency Reader: *I Can See*
- My Alphabet Book, p. 5
- My Read and Write Book, p. 14

 The Big Book is available on audiocassette in the Literacy Place Listening Center.

My Alphabet Book, p. 5

Revisit the Big Book

Consonant /k/c

ⒶPHONOLOGICAL AWARENESS

Oral Blending Read the following word parts, and ask children to blend them to make a word. Provide corrective feedback and modeling as required.

/k/. . . an	/k/. . . ap	/k/. . . at
/k/. . . ake	/k/. . . ook	/k/. . . atch

ⒷCONNECT SOUND-SPELLING

Introduce Consonant /k/c Flip through *Apples, Alligators and also Alphabets* until you get to the *Cc* page. Point out that the letter *Cc* stands for **/k/** as in *cats*.

- Ask children to say the **/k/** sound with you.
- Say the names of the animals and objects on the page and ask children to exaggerate **/k/** at the beginning of each name.

Point to the ABC card for *Cc* and have children name the letter and picture, exaggerating the **/k/** at the beginning of the picture name.

Letter Formation

WRITE THE LETTER

Write *Cc* on the chalkboard or on chart paper. Point out the capital and small forms of the letter. Model how to write the letter using the rhyme provided.

- Have children write the letter in the air with their fingers. Ask children to make the letter's sound as they practice writing.
- Note how children position their paper and grip their pencil when they write.

Cc

Begin like a circle, around to the side,
(Curve around to the left in a semicircle.)
But stop and leave its mouth open wide.

Reread the Big Book

OPTIONS

Sequence Story Events Before you begin rereading *I Went Walking,* invite children to explain in their own words what happens in the book. As you reread, ask children to note the order in which each animal is introduced, and the different pieces of clothing that the child loses.

Choral Reading Have one group of children read the repeated statement *I went walking.* Have another group read the repeated question *What did you see?* Invite both groups to provide the answers together.

Decoding Strategies As you reread the story, point out to children that they can use the letters and sounds they have learned to figure out words. Stop before words that begin with **/a/a, /b/b,** and **/k/c** *(cat, cow, brown, black, animals).*

Point to the first letter of the word and have children say the sound. Help children use the letter-sound relationship, picture clues, and story pattern to read the words.

READ AND WRITE INDEPENDENTLY

Journal Place copies of *I Went Walking* in the Reading Center for children to read on their own or in small groups. Invite children to write in their Journals about a special walk they've taken.

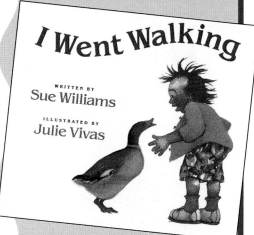

I Went Walking

Concepts of Print

PERIODS AND QUESTION MARKS

Turn to the first page that says: *I went walking. What did you see?*

- Read the first sentence and then point to the period. Explain that this mark is called a period and that it tells that a sentence has ended.

- Read the second sentence and then point to the question mark. Explain that this is called a question mark and it also tells that a sentence has ended.

- Point out that question marks only come at the end of questions.

- Demonstrate how to read a question by changing the intonation in your voice. Invite volunteers to think of questions and to say them with expression.

- Reread the book together. Invite children to point to the periods and question marks. Encourage them to read with the appropriate expression.

MODIFY Instruction

ESL/ELD

▲ Have children review the names of all the animals that have followed the girl, using words like *first, next,* and *then.* Then turn to the last page and discuss what the children think the girl might do now that she realizes that all the animals have followed her. **(PREDICT)**

DAY 3

I Can See

My Read and Write Book, p. 14

Read High-Frequency Reader

INTRODUCE THE BOOK

Show the book *I Can See*. Read the title and the author's name. Explain that the book shows photographs of real animals and where they live.

▶ **What are some of your favorite animals? Where do these animals live?**

▶ **What animals do you think will be in this book?**

HIGH-FREQUENCY WORDS: *a, can*

- Write the sentence stem *I can see a* _____ on the board. Underline the word *can.* Then write the word *can* on a note card. Read it aloud.
- Display the card and have children read the word.
- Help children spell it aloud, clapping on each letter.
- Ask children to write it in the air as they state aloud each letter.

Repeat with the word *a.* Review the high-frequency words *I* and *see.* Ask volunteers to find each on the Word Wall.

Invite children to complete the sentence stem by naming something that they might see on a walk. Write each new sentence on the board.

Add the cards for *can* and *a* to the Word Wall.

SHARE THE HIGH-FREQUENCY READER

Read the story aloud, tracking the print. Invite children to point to the high-frequency words *can* and *a.*

- After each two-page spread, ask: *Have you ever seen this animal?* Encourage children to share the place they saw each animal.
- This story also reviews consonant /b/b. Help children use their knowledge of this sound-spelling to decode words.

SHARED WRITING

Invite children to make a class book called *I Can See*.

- Ask each child to think of an animal. Help children write and complete the sentence *I can see a* _____ with the name of the animal they have chosen and the animal's color.
- Have children illustrate their sentences. Encourage them to include clues about where they might find their animal. Bind the pages into a class book.

CENTER WORKSHOPS

Games

Do You Have a Clue?

Place a variety of objects in boxes or bags. Invite partners to play a guessing game. Guide one child to select and describe an object.

Encourage children to provide as many descriptive clues as possible such as colors, texture, and shape to help their partner. Partners can take turns describing and guessing the objects.

Observation: Notice how children use the clues to solve the problem. What other strategies are they using?

MATERIALS

- Objects with a variety of shapes, sizes and colors, such as pencils, pattern blocks, and toys
- Box or bag

Art

Color Collages

Invite children to work in small groups to create a collage on a large piece of oaktag.

- Place cardboard boxes in the Art Center. Label each box with the name of a color. Ask children to put things in each box that can be used for a collage.

- Children can contribute items from home, such as beads and plastic lids, or found items such as leaves and flower petals.

Children can choose one color and complete their collage by drawing or painting in that color. Have children write the name of the color somewhere on the collage.

Observation: Notice how children create their collages.

MATERIALS

- Oaktag
- Colored paper
- Markers, crayons
- Paints, scissors, glue
- Collage materials (crepe paper, pipe cleaners, sequins, confetti, macaroni)
- Old magazines

Share the Read Aloud

DAY 4

DAY 4 OBJECTIVES

CHILDREN WILL:

- listen for /k/
- review consonant /k/c
- read and respond to *Caps for Sale*
- recognize repetitive language
- explore problem solving
- write describing words
- engage in Center Workshops

MATERIALS

- *Caps for Sale*
- My Read and Write Book, p. 15

TECHNOLOGY

 Children might enjoy viewing the film *Caps for Sale*, available from Weston Woods.

DAILY PHONICS

Consonant /k/c

Ⓐ PHONOLOGICAL AWARENESS

Oddity Task: Beginning Sounds Invite children to play a matching game using the picture cards for *cat, coat, cup, bee, bus,* and *bat.* Tell them to mix up the cards and place each card on the table, face down. Direct children to take turns turning over two cards at a time, saying the picture words, and telling whether or not they begin with the same sound.

Ⓑ CONNECT SOUND-SPELLING

A Cow Coughs Write *cat* on the board, and circle the **c.** Remind children that the letter *c* stands for **/k/.** Invite them to suggest words that begin with **/k/.** Write them on the board, and have volunteers circle the letter *c* in those words containing this spelling for **/k/.**

Then invite the group to think of sentences with two or more **/k/c** words that they can act out. For example: *A cold cow coughs; The cat combs its hair.*

Build Background

ORAL LANGUAGE: PEDDLERS

Ask children where people go to buy things.

▶ **Where do people buy food? clothes?**

Ask children to consider where people bought the things they needed when there weren't any stores to shop in. Share with children that long ago people bought many of their things from peddlers. Explain that a peddler is like a salesperson in a store but moves from place to place.

PREVIEW AND PREDICT

Display the front cover of *Caps for Sale.* Read the title and the author/illustrator's name.

▶ **Why do you think the man is in the tree?**

▶ **What could the caps be doing at the bottom?**

Share the Read Aloud

RECOGNIZE REPETITIVE LANGUAGE

Invite children to participate actively in the story. They may begin by chiming in when they hear the chant, "Caps! Caps for sale! Fifty cents a cap!" and the predictable refrain, "You monkeys, you! You give me back my caps."

As you read the story emphasize some of the other words and phrases that are repeated so that children get a sense of the rhythm of the language.

Caps for Sale

Respond to the Literature

TALK ABOUT IT

Share Personal Responses Read the phrase below the title on the title page:

"A tale of a peddler, some monkeys and their monkey business." Discuss what "monkey business" means in this story.

▶ **How do you think the peddler felt when the monkeys took his caps?**

▶ **How would you feel if you were the peddler? Has anyone ever teased you?**

▶ **How did that make you feel?**

THINK ABOUT IT

Explore Problem Solving Ask children to recall the characters in the story.

▶ **Which character had a problem? What was the problem?**

▶ **How did the peddler solve his problem?**

▶ **Can you think of other ways the peddler could have solved his problem?**

ESL/ELD

▲ As some English language learners chime in on the predictable refrain, other English language learners might pantomime the actions of the peddler and the monkeys. **(PANTOMIME)**

MODIFY Instruction

GIFTED & TALENTED

✳ Challenge children to "pretend" to organize a market where they can sell goods. In small groups, children can discuss the kinds of caps or other goods they would like to sell, the price of the goods, how to attract customers, and what makes a good location. **(WORK IN GROUPS)**

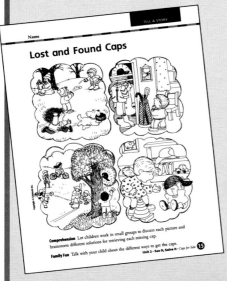

My Read and Write Book, p. 15

Shared Writing

WRITE DESCRIBING WORDS

Invite children to draw caps on a chart, using the colors and designs mentioned in the book—a red cap, a grey cap, a checked cap, a brown cap, and a blue cap.

Ask children to help write descriptions of the caps next to their drawings. Children can write the letters that stand for the sounds they know. Ask them to point to and read the descriptive words.

Work with children to make sure their text is moving from left to right and from top to bottom.

Repeated Reading

ADD STORY MOVEMENTS

Before rereading the story, revisit the illustrations. Ask children to recall how the peddler reacted each time the monkeys ignored him. Point out opportunities for children to express the text through movement (stamping feet, shaking a finger, shaking hands, throwing the cap down).

Reread the story, encouraging children to chime in with words and movement.

READ AND WRITE INDEPENDENTLY

Journal Place copies of *Caps for Sale* in the Reading Center so that children may enjoy the story independently or with a friend. Encourage children to write and draw in their Journals about their favorite part of the story.

✓ Comprehension Check

RETELL THE STORY

Guide children to retell the story using the illustrations to help them recall the main events. Encourage them to tell how the peddler is feeling, what the problem is and how the peddler solves the problem at the end of the story.

CENTER WORKSHOPS

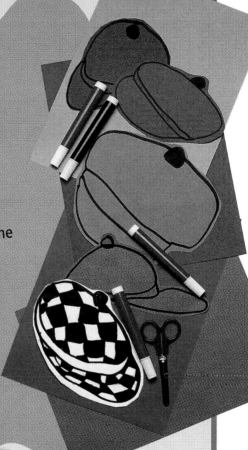

The Peddler's Caps

Invite children to recreate a scene from *Caps for Sale* using clay to mold the peddler and construction paper for the caps. Have them place caps on the peddler's head in the order described in the book. Provide a copy of the story so children can refer to it.

MATERIALS

- Multi-colored clay
- Tree branches
- Empty, clean tuna cans
- Construction paper in cap shapes
- *Caps for Sale*

- Children can support a small tree branch in a tuna can with clay, and add clay monkeys in the tree and construction paper caps on the monkeys' heads.

- Children can count the number of each kind of colored cap and the number of caps in all.

Observation: How do children recreate this scene?

Monkey See, Monkey Do!

Share the expression "Monkey see, monkey do!" Ask if any children have seen monkeys mimic one another in a zoo.

Children will enjoy mimicking partners, as the monkeys did to the frustrated peddler. Add hats or caps for additional fun to be had by the "monkeys."

MATERIALS

- Felt or colored construction paper for hats or caps

Observation: Notice which children particularly respond to this activity.

Sounds and Letters

DAILY PHONICS

Consonant /k/c

A PHONOLOGICAL AWARENESS

Auditory Discrimination Recite the poem "Little Boy Blue" from the *Big Book of Rhymes and Rhythms*. Invite children familiar with the rhyme to say it along with you. Then recite the rhyme again, emphasizing the beginning sound in *come*, *cow's*, and *corn*. Ask children to name the letter that stands for the sound **/k/.**

Big Book of Rhymes and Rhythms, p. 8

B CONCEPTS OF PRINT

Place the *Big Book of Rhymes and Rhythms*, the Sentence Strips for "Little Boy Blue," and a pocket chart in the Reading Center. Then do the following:

- Cover all *Cc* words with index cards or sticky notes.
- As you sing the rhyme together, stop at the words that are covered and provide an opportunity for children to predict text and to focus on words that begin with **/k/.**
- Unmask each word after accepting children's predictions. Let children use the Sentence Strips to assemble the rhyme in a pocket chart as you read it aloud again.

| Little Boy Blue, |
| Come blow your horn. |
| The sheep's in the meadow, |
| The cow's in the corn. |

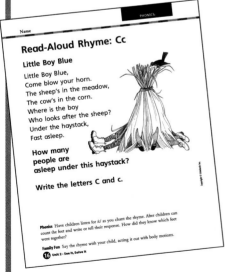

My Read and Write Book, p. 16

For additional practice see *Scholastic Phonics K,* pp. 19–22. Also see Sound and Letter Book: *I Can See . . . .*

EXTRA HELP

■ Set out magnetic letters, sponge letters, plastic letters and any other letters you have collected. Invite children to think of *Cc* words. Write the words on the chalkboard. Ask volunteers to find a *Cc* from the alphabet materials and match it to the initial *c* in the word. **(HANDS-ON LEARNING)**

C CONNECT SOUND-SPELLING

Alphabetic Principle Remind children that the letter *c* stands for **/k/** as in *cat*. Display the cover of *Caps for Sale*. Ask children to find the word that begins with the **/k/** sound. Point out the capital *C* at the beginning of *Caps*. Read the word in the context of the title.

ABC Book Explain to children that they are going to make a new page for their own ABC book. Have children make suggestions of animals, objects, and people whose names begin with **/k/.** When the list is complete, invite children to work together to create the *Cc* page for their ABC books.

Carol Goes to Camp Have children sit in a circle to play "Carol Goes to Camp." Explain that everything Carol takes to camp begins with **/k/.** Begin by saying *Carol goes to camp and takes a comb.* The next player repeats the sentence and adds another item whose name begins with **/k/.** Write the words on the chalkboard as children name them. Have volunteers underline the initial *c* in the words that begin with *c*. Explain that the letter *k* also stands for the **/k/** sound.

D VOCABULARY: HIGH-FREQUENCY WORDS

Write the sentence ***I can see a cat*** on the chalkboard. Read the sentence aloud and then do the following.

• Review the high-frequency words *I, can, see,* and *a*. If necessary, use the read-spell-write routine for each word.

• Make word cards for *can, see, I,* and *a*.

• Pick a card and give clues so that children can guess the word. For example: *This word has three letters. It starts with a c.* Have children guess which word is on your card. Show the card and have children read it.

• Invite children to pick cards and give clues to the class.

TECHNOLOGY

 Have children write *CA* several times on the **WiggleWorks Plus** Magnet Board. Help children add one letter to make words as shown above.

The rhyme in the *Big Book of Rhymes and Rhythms* is available on the **Sounds of Phonics** audiocassette.

Getting Ready

MODIFY
Instruction

ESL/ELD

▲ Ask: *What do you do in the morning to get ready?* Then invite partners to act out the story *Getting Ready.* Provide props such as a sock, shoe, brush, sweater, coat, and mitten. **(ACT IT OUT)**

Read My Book

INTRODUCE THE BOOK
Let children know that they are going to get their own book that they can read on their own and take home.

▶ **What kinds of things do you do each morning to get ready for school?**

PREVIEW AND PREDICT
Pass out copies of *Getting Ready.* Read the title and the author's and illustrator's names. Ask children about the illustration on the cover.

▶ **What do you think this book might be about?**

READ TOGETHER
Read the My Book with children tracking print as you read. Guide children to read along in their copies and to point out the ways the dog helps the boy get ready for his day.

PHONICS
Ask children to find the word *coat* and say it aloud.

▶ **What letter do you see at the beginning of the word?**

▶ **What sound does that letter stand for?**

READ AND WRITE INDEPENDENTLY
Journal Encourage children to read *Getting Ready* on their own or in small groups. Provide crayons and invite children to color the illustrations.

HOME/SCHOOL CONNECTION
Children can take home their My Books to share with family members and friends. Suggest that children make books with family members about their morning routine.

CENTER WORKSHOPS

A Case of Carrots!

Bring in several bunches of carrots with the greens still attached if possible. Talk together about how carrots grow underground.

- Write the word *carrot* on oaktag or index cards and give a card to each child. Let children discover that the word *carrot* begins with the letter that stands for **/k/**.

- If you give them safety tips and practice, children can wash and peel the carrots with vegetable peelers or plastic knives. Then they can eat the carrots.

- While they are working, encourage children to think of other food names they know that begin with **/k/**. List these on a chart. Include *corn, cake,* and *cookies*.

Observation: As they peel their carrots, listen to what children talk about for clues to their understanding of initial *Cc*.

MATERIALS

- Bunch of carrots
- Dull vegetable peelers or plastic knives
- Oaktag or index cards with the word *carrot* on them
- Sorting cards

Are You Ready?

Encourage children to pretend to be different people getting ready in the morning. They can be people in their families or other people like firefighters, doctors, or those who have jobs that require them to wear special uniforms.

Invite children to make up short scenes that show the different kinds of things people might do to get ready for their day.

Observation: Notice how children engage in imaginary role-play and work together to create a scene.

MATERIALS

- Dress-up clothes

DAY 6 OBJECTIVES

CHILDREN WILL:

- recognize /d/
- read and respond to *Boots*
- talk about weather and clothing
- recognize story pattern
- engage in Center Workshops

MATERIALS

- *Boots*
- **My Read and Write Book,** pp. 17–18

GUIDED READING

To conclude each day's reading session, meet with guided reading groups. You might use Scholastic's Guided Reading Library or other books in your library.

TECHNOLOGY

 Children can interact with the **WiggleWorks Plus** selection on the computer. Ask children to use the My Book version of the story to color the pictures. Encourage them to rewrite the text.

 The song is available on the **Sounds of Phonics** audiocassette.

Share the WiggleWorks Book

DAILY PHONICS

Consonant /d/d

PHONOLOGICAL AWARENESS

Rhyme Sing or say the nursery rhyme "Hey, Diddle, Diddle" emphasizing the initial /d/ in the words *diddle, dog,* and *dish.* Repeat the title of the rhyme and ask children to say the sound they hear at the beginning of the word *diddle.*

- Repeat the rhyme. Have children clap every time they hear a word that begins with **/d/.**
- Invite children to join you as you say it again.

Hey, Diddle, Diddle

Hey, diddle, diddle
The cat and the fiddle
The cow jumped over the moon,
The little dog laughed to see such sport
And the dish ran away with the spoon.

Build Background

ORAL LANGUAGE: WEATHER

Take children outside. When you come back, ask children to describe today's weather using weather words such as *sunny, rainy, cold,* or *windy.* Discuss the different kinds of weather, including changes in temperature, types of storms, and seasonal changes. Create a chart of weather words.

PREVIEW AND PREDICT

Show children the cover of *Boots,* pointing out the title and the author's and illustrator's names. Ask children what they think will happen.

SET A PURPOSE

Point to the different clothes items on the book cover's border. Invite children to look for each item in the book.

Read the WiggleWorks Book

POINT TO THE WORDS

Open the book and ask children what they think is happening in the first picture. How do they know that the class is getting ready to go out?

Read the book, emphasizing the cumulative pattern. Invite children to notice each new item of clothing in the pictures and to join in on the repeated clothing words. Before turning to the last page, ask:

▶ **What do you think will happen now that the boy is ready to go out?**

As you read, track the words with your finger, modeling the left-to-right progression.

Boots

Respond to the Literature

TALK ABOUT IT

Share Personal Responses Ask children if they thought the book was funny. Encourage them to have conversations with one another, explaining their answers.

▶ **What was the boy doing throughout the book?**

▶ **Why did it take him longer that anyone else?**

Ask children if something similar to what happened to the boy has ever happened to them.

THINK ABOUT IT

Add Clothes to the Weather Chart Together go through the book and note the different clothes the boy wore to go outside in the cold.

• Invite children to think about the different kinds of clothes they wear in different weather conditions. Read the list of weather words made during Build Background.

• Have children draw appropriate clothes next to each weather word.

hot

snow

rain

MODIFY Instruction

ESL/ELD

▲ Go over the weather words from the Build Background activity. Ask: *When do you wear _____?* If possible, bring real articles of clothing or draw pictures to help children acquiring English learn the names of the clothing mentioned in *Boots*. **(USE PICTURES)**

TECHNOLOGY

Invite children to think about clothing for a season other than winter. Have them open the **WiggleWorks Plus** My Book version of the story and model the pattern of the book in writing names of items they would wear. Then have them write on the screen the name of the season.

TECHNOLOGY

 Invite children to use the **WiggleWorks Plus** Record and Playback tools to retell the book in a simple narrative style. Encourage them to play back their retelling and to compare it with the original to decide which one they like better.

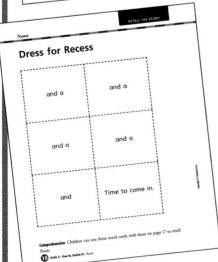

My Read and Write Book, pp. 17–18

Shared Writing

WRITE A CUMULATIVE STORY

Write the word "Boots" on a chart. Recalling the pattern of the story, write on the next line the phrase "Boots and a sweater." Ask children to help you add the lines from the story by writing the letters that stand for the sounds they know. Invite children to draw the clothing too. Point out that the words in a story are written from left to right.

> Boots
>
> Boots and a sweater
> Boots and a sweater and a hat.
> Boots and a sweater
> and a hat and a scarf.
> Boots and a sweater and a hat
> and a scarf and a coat.

Repeated Reading

FOCUS ON PREDICTION

Reread *Boots* with children. As you do, ask them to predict what the boy will put on next. Ask children how they remembered what came next.

▶ **How did you solve the problem of figuring out the words?**

▶ **How do the pictures help you figure out the boy is going to be the last one ready to go out?**

READ AND WRITE INDEPENDENTLY

Journal Children can read *Boots* on their own or in small groups. In their Journals children can draw, in cartoon squares, pictures of themselves getting dressed for outdoors. Children can write about their drawings.

☑ Comprehension Check

ACT IT OUT

Children can work in small groups to act out this story. Provide dress-up props that children request.

CENTER WORKSHOPS

Self-Portrait

Invite children to draw pictures of themselves dressed for a snowy or rainy day.

Children can use story words and other words to label each item of clothing in their pictures.

Observation: How do children portray themselves?

MATERIALS

- Paper
- Pencils
- Crayons

Writing Sentences

Encourage children to complete one or more of these sentences to write a personal response to the book. They can write the sentences in their Journals or on a piece of paper. Invite children to illustrate their responses.

When I go out, I wear _____ .

Once I was last because _____ .

When it's cold out, I put on _____ .

I like to wear boots because _____ .

Invite children to share their sentences and drawings.

Observation: How do children complete the sentence?

MATERIALS

- Pencils
- Paper
- Crayons

When it's cold out I

DAY 7 OBJECTIVES

CHILDREN WILL:

- listen for alliteration
- recognize /d/d and write *Dd*
- demonstrate visual literacy
- use a map
- revisit High-Frequency Reader: *I Can See*
- review the high-frequency words
- engage in Center Workshops

MATERIALS

- *Apples, Alligators and also Alphabets*
- *Problem Solving,* SourceCard 2
- High-Frequency Reader: *I Can See*
- My Alphabet Book, p. 6

TECHNOLOGY

 Encourage children to use the drawing and writing tools in the **WiggleWorks Plus** Write area to complete the activities in this lesson.

My Alphabet Book, p. 6

Read the SourceCard

 DAILY PHONICS

 and Read the High-Frequency Reader

Consonant /d/d

Ⓐ PHONOLOGICAL AWARENESS

Alliteration Write the following alliterative sentence on the chalkboard:

Do dogs dig down deep?

Read aloud the sentence and have children repeat it. Then ask children to count the number of times they hear **/d/** in the sentence. Invite children to suggest other words that begin with **/d/.**

Ⓑ CONNECT SOUND-SPELLING

Introduce Consonant /d/d Page through *Apples, Alligators and also Alphabets* saying each letter name until you get to the *Dd* page. Point out that the letter *Dd* stands for **/d/** as in **dinosaur.**

- Say the names of the animals and objects on the page and ask children to exaggerate **/d/** at the beginning of each name.

Letter Formation

WRITE THE LETTER

Write *Dd* on the chalkboard. Point out the capital and small forms of the letter.

- Have children write both forms of the letter in the air or in sand with their fingers. Ask children to make the letter's sound as they practice writing. Use the rhymes below as you demonstrate how the letters are formed.

D	d
Little Duck swims in a straight line down, *(Pull down straight.)* Then flies back and circles around. *(Retrace up, circle right.)*	Go straight down and halfway back, *(Pull down straight. Retrace part way.)* Now circle left and return to the track. *(Circle left.)*

Share the SourceCard

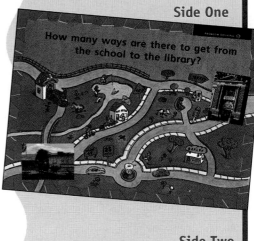

Side One

SIDE ONE   **Read a Map** Guide children to look at the map of the town on the SourceCard.

> ▶ **Do you see the school? Do you see the library? How can you get from the school to the library?**

Ask a volunteer to use his or her finger to trace a route from the school to the library.

Read the question, "How many ways are there to get from the school to the library?" Invite other children to trace different routes from the school to the library. Together, count the number of different routes.

Side Two

SIDE TWO   **Explore Shoes We Wear** Read the question "When would you wear these shoes?" on side two of the SourceCard. Invite children to name the times and places they might wear the different shoes.

> ▶ **Which kind of shoes have you worn?**

> ▶ **Which shoes are everyday shoes? Which shoes are meant to be worn on special occasions?**

Shared Writing

WRITE PLACE NAMES   Ask children to look on the map on the SourceCard to find another place in the town they might like to visit. Write the following question on a chart, filling in the blanks with the names of two places. Invite children to write the letters that stand for the sounds they know.

• Encourage children to answer the question by tracing the different routes.

How many ways are there to get from the _____ to the _____ ?

MODIFY Instruction

ESL/ELD

▲ To help English language learners participate in the discussion about ways to go from one place to another, provide a set of labeled pictures of cars, buses, subways, and pedestrians. Help children pronounce each word and guide them to formulate phrases by suggesting words such as *from, to,* and *by.* **(USE PICTURES)**

I Can See

MODIFY Instruction

EXTRA HELP

■ Have children study the animals in *I Can See*. Ask them if they have ever seen any of these animals before. Have they seen them in books? In a zoo? In a park? You may wish to make a chart on the chalkboard listing the names of the animals and the children who have seen them. **(MAKE CONNECTIONS)**

Revisit High-Frequency Reader

REREAD THE BOOK

Invite children to join you as you read *I Can See* again. On the first page, have children read the high-frequency words *I, can,* and *see*. Review these words.

DECODING STRATEGIES

As you read the book, point to each word, the picture clue, the initial letter, and any other sound-spellings children have learned. Pause long enough for children to read before you do. Model blending words as needed. For example, have children use their knowledge of **/b/b** and the picture to decode *bear, brown,* and *black*.

Think Aloud *At the beginning of the word, I see the letter* b. *I know that* b *stands for* **/b/.** *In the picture, I see a bear. The word* bear *begins with* **/b/.** *This word is* bear. *That makes sense in this sentence.*

CONCEPTS OF PRINT: WORDS

Give small groups of children sentence strips for the story. Invite them to match the strips to the pages in the book. Have them count the words in each sentence.

> I can see a red ladybug.

> I can see a brown bear.

ORAL LANGUAGE: COLOR WORDS

Name a color from the book and ask children to name something in the classroom that matches that color or something that is always that color.

READ FOR FLUENCY

Give each child their own copy of *I Can See*. Have children read their books with a partner. Partners may want to alternate reading each page. After they finish the page, they can pretend to be the animal in the photograph.

READ AND WRITE INDEPENDENTLY

Journal Place copies of the High-Frequency Reader in the Reading Center for children to read on their own. Children can draw a favorite animal and write its name and color in their Journals.

HOME/SCHOOL CONNECTION

Children can take home their High-Frequency Reader and take a walk through a park or wooded area with family members to observe what they can.

CENTER WORKSHOPS

Drawing a Town

Place copies of *Caps for Sale* and the SourceCard in the Art Center. Invite children to draw pictures of places found in a town, using the book, SourceCard, or their own experiences for ideas. Ask children to draw each place on a separate piece of paper.

Write "Our Town" on a large piece of mural paper. After children finish drawing, they can cut out their pictures and glue them to the mural.

Encourage children to label the places in the town. Then ask if children can think of any other places that should be included.

Observation: Which children are particularly interested in drawing maps? Provide more time for them to work on their murals.

MATERIALS

- Mural paper
- Paper
- Crayons, paints
- Scissors, glue
- *Caps for Sale*
- *Problem Solving SourceCard 2*

MATERIALS

- A variety of shoes
- Paper
- Crayons

If the Shoe Fits

Place shoes of different styles, sizes, and colors in a large box. Encourage children to match the shoes to make pairs and to sort the shoes into categories by their attributes.

- Invite children to draw pictures of themselves wearing the shoes and doing an activity that the shoes suggest to them.

Observation: How do children categorize the shoes?

DAY 8 OBJECTIVES

CHILDREN WILL:

- orally blend onset and rime
- review consonant /d/d
- read and respond to *Carlos and the Squash Plant*
- compare language in different countries
- write a recipe
- recognize fantasy and reality
- engage in Center Workshops

MATERIALS

- *Carlos and the Squash Plant*
- *My Read and Write Book,* p. 19

Share the Read Aloud

DAILY PHONICS

Consonant /d/d

Ⓐ PHONOLOGICAL AWARENESS

Oral Blending State aloud the following word parts, and ask children to blend them. Model as necessary.

/d/ . . . ate	/d/ . . . og	/d/ . . . irt
/d/ . . . esk	/d/ . . . id	/d/ . . . ark

Ⓑ CONNECT SOUND-SPELLING

Doors, Ducks, and Doughnuts Write the word *door* on an index card, underline the *d,* and attach it to a door. Remind children that the letter *Dd* stands for /d/ as in *door*. Invite children to suggest words that begin with /d/. Help them write each word on an index card and attach it to the door. Read the /d/d words and have volunteers underline the letter *Dd* in each.

Build Background

ORAL LANGUAGE: KEEPING CLEAN

Ask children to talk about some of the things they do to keep clean.

▶ **What kinds of things do you use to get clean?**

▶ **Why is it important to get clean?**

▶ **What are some things that are fun about getting clean?**

▶ **What are some things that aren't so much fun about getting clean?**

PREVIEW AND PREDICT

Read the title of the book and the author's and illustrator's names in both English and Spanish. Point out that this book is written in two languages so that more children can enjoy it. Then ask:

▶ **What do you think the boy on the cover is doing?**

▶ **Where do you think this story takes place? Why?**

Share the Read Aloud

FOCUS ON PLOT

Read the book in one sitting, pausing after each page to allow time for children to look at the colorful illustrations.

- As you read, encourage children to use the pictures on each page to describe what is happening in the story and how Carlos is behaving and changing.

- Children might enjoy participating actively by mimicking Carlos's facial expression as the story events unfold.

Invite children to notice the Spanish portion of the text. If there are Spanish speaking children in your class, you might also want to read the Spanish version. Encourage them to notice differences in the two versions.

Carlos and the Squash Plant

Respond to the Literature

TALK ABOUT IT

Share Personal Responses Encourage children to share their reactions to the story. Help them clarify their ideas about which story events are imaginary and which are real.

▶ **What was your favorite part of the story?**

▶ **Why did the squash plant grow out of Carlos's ear?**

▶ **Which parts of the story do you think could really have happened?**

▶ **Which parts of the story do you think are imaginary?**

THINK ABOUT IT

Discuss Languages and Culture Show a page from *Carlos and the Squash Plant* and have children identify the English and Spanish portions of the text. Point out that where Carlos lives, there are many people who speak both Spanish and English.

- Have children talk about different languages. Invite them to share phrases from languages they know.

- Together go through the story and talk about the Spanish words and phrases in the English version, such as *Si, Mama, calabacitas,* or *Ay, caramba.* Have Spanish speaking children share what these phrases mean.

MODIFY Instruction

ESL/ELD

▲ Invite children to discuss whether they are familiar with any of the foods mentioned in *Carlos and the Squash Plant.* Ask them to tell about their favorite foods. **(MAKE CONNECTIONS)**

DAY 8

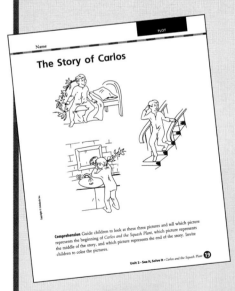

The Story of Carlos

Comprehension Guide children to look at these three pictures and tell which picture represents the beginning of *Carlos and the Squash Plant*, which picture represents the middle of the story, and which picture represents the end of the story. Invite children to color the pictures.

Unit 2 - See It, Solve It - *Carlos and the Squash Plant* 19

My Read and Write Book, p. 19

Shared Writing

WRITE A RECIPE

Ask children if they have ever used a recipe. Discuss how a recipe has two parts—a list of ingredients and directions for how to use them. Ask children to recall the special food that was mentioned in the story.

• Show children the recipe for *calabacitas* at the back of the book and point out the list of ingredients and the directions.

• Help children write a class recipe for something that is simple and familiar, or suggest that the class make up a fun recipe for a sandwich that includes many ingredients.

• Have children suggest ideas for ingredients to include in their sandwich. Help them write the ingredients on chart paper using the letters they know.

• They may also wish to include a picture.

• Then write the directions. Discuss why a recipe has to follow a certain sequence.

Repeated Reading

RECOGNIZE FANTASY AND REALITY

Revisit the story and talk about which parts could not really happen, and why. Explain that authors sometimes make up imaginary things to put in a book to make it fun to read. Discuss how the story would be different if the squash plant didn't grow out of the boy's ear.

READ AND WRITE INDEPENDENTLY

Journal Place *Carlos and the Squash Plant* in the Reading Center so children can read it independently. Invite children to imagine something that they could not really do or that could not really happen to them and to draw and write about it in their Journals.

✅ Comprehension Check

RETELL THE STORY

Invite children to retell the story as you ask questions.

▶ **What did Carlos not want to do?**

▶ **What happened because Carlos didn't want to take a bath?**

▶ **How did Carlos hide the squash plant in his ear?**

▶ **How did Carlos get rid of the squash plant?**

CENTER WORKSHOPS

MATERIALS

- **Different kinds of dirt such as soil, sand, small rocks, and pebbles**
- **Strainer**
- **Scale**
- **Chart paper**
- **Small toys**

Explore Dirt

Ask children to think of questions they have about dirt. List their questions on chart paper. Collect dirt and invite children to experiment. You may want to make a list of the different components of dirt such as pieces of leaves, twigs, pebbles, and finer sand. You may wish to have them compare sand with dirt and note the differences.

- Encourage them to weigh dirt when it is dry and then when it is wet.
- In a chart, record observations about the smell, feel, and weight of dirt.

Observation: Notice the different ways children explore dirt and how they explain their observations.

MATERIALS

- **Washcloths**
- **Plastic dishes**
- **Dolls with hair**
- **Paint brush**
- **Pieces of wood**
- **Water table or basin filled with water**
- **Chart paper**

Wash and Dry!

Set up a water table, or a basin filled with water, in which children can wash a variety of objects. Designate a drying area where objects can dry and encourage children to check to see which objects dried the fastest.

▶ **Which object took the longest to dry?**

▶ **Which objects dried the quickest?**

Encourage children to notice what the objects they are experimenting with are made of, such as plastic, cloth, or wood. Make a picture chart of your experiments.

Observation: Notice how children observe differences in drying times.

DAY 9 OBJECTIVES

CHILDREN WILL:

- recognize /d/ *d*
- recognize rhyming words
- read a rhyme
- connect speaking and writing
- review high-frequency words
- read My Book: *Time to Get Up!*
- engage in Center Workshops

MATERIALS

- *Big Book of Rhymes and Rhythms,* p. 9
- ABC Card: *Dd*
- *Darlene*
- *I Went Walking*
- My Book: *Time to Get Up!*
- Sentence Strips for *Hickory, Dickory, Dock!*
- *My Read and Write Book,* p. 20

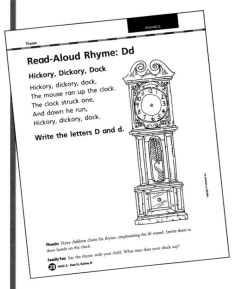

My Read and Write Book, p. 20

For additional practice, see *Scholastic Phonics K,* pp. 23–27. Also see Sound and Letter Book: *We Like Dogs.*

Sounds and Letters

and Read My Book

Consonant /d/ *d*

Ⓐ PHONOLOGICAL AWARENESS

Rhyme Read the title of the rhyme "Hickory, Dickory, Dock" from the *Big Book of Rhymes and Rhythms.* Say the words *Dickory* and *Dock* slowly, emphasizing the beginning sound. Recite "Hickory, Dickory, Dock," inviting children to join in as you read.

Have each child write *Dd* on a card. As you reread the rhyme, guide children to listen for words that begin with **/d/.** Have children hold up their *Dd* cards when they hear a word beginning with **/d/** and then say the word.

Read the rhyme again. This time, ask children to raise their hands when they hear words that rhyme with "dock" and "one."

Big Book of Rhymes and Rhythms, p. 9

Ⓑ CONCEPTS OF PRINT

Display the sentence strips for "Hickory, Dickory, Dock" in a pocket chart, and guide children to form five groups. Give a sentence strip to each group.

- Tell children to find words that begin with *Dd* and to cover them with sticky notes.
- Sing the song again line by line. Pause while children place their strip back into the pocket chart.
- When the strips are back in order, reread the rhyme together. Let the children figure out each covered word, and then remove the sticky note.

Hickory, dickory, dock,

The mouse ran up the clock.

The clock struck one,

And down he run.

Hickory, dickory, dock.

MODIFY
Instruction

© CONNECT SOUND-SPELLING

Alphabetic Principle Point to the *Dd* ABC Card and have children name the letter and picture. Encourage them to say the **/d/** sound. Have them point to any other words around the room that begin with *Dd*.

- Remind children of the book they read about Darlene. Ask a child to point out the *D* in *Darlene* on the cover of the book.

- Next, open *I Went Walking* to the page about the green duck. Have children find the word that begins with *d*. Read it together.

- Finally, invite children whose names begin with *D* to stand next to their name cards.

ABC Book Explain to children that they are going to make a new page for their own ABC book. Have children suggest animals, objects, and people whose names begin with **/d/.** When the list is complete, invite children to work together to create the *Dd* page for their ABC books.

***Dd* Animal Bulletin Board** The names of many animals begin with *Dd*. Children can draw pictures of deer, dogs, ducks, dolphins, and donkeys and label them for an animal bulletin board.

◑ VOCABULARY: HIGH-FREQUENCY WORDS

Write the incomplete sentence *I can see a* _____ on the chalkboard. Read it aloud together and review the high-frequency words. Then do the following:

- Write the word **cat** in the blank space. Say the word and have children read the new sentence.

- Repeat with the word **bat.**

- Invite children to think of words that rhyme with **cat** and **bat.** Let them see if they make sense in the sentence.

ESL/ELD

▲ English language learners might benefit from recording words that begin with the letter *Dd*. Help partners record the words with *Dd*, then let them listen to the words they recorded. This activity will help children practice pronunciation and improve vocabulary. **(USE AUDIO)**

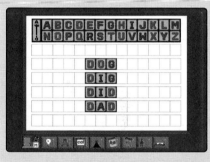

TECHNOLOGY

 Place Sentence Strips for "Hickory, Dickory, Dock" beside the **WiggleWorks Plus** Magnet Board. Children can find and create words that begin with the /d/ sound. For additional practice with words that begin with *Dd*, ask children to write the words shown above.

 The rhyme in the *Big Book of Rhymes and Rhythms* is available on the **Sounds of Phonics** audiocassette.

Time to Get Up!

ESL/ELD

▲ Encourage English language learners to discuss how they are woken up in the morning. (MAKE CONNECTIONS)

Read My Book

INTRODUCE THE BOOK

Let children know that they are going to get their own book that they can read on their own and take home.

▶ **Have you ever had to try many different ways to solve a problem before you could do it?**

▶ **How did it make you feel?**

PREVIEW AND PREDICT

Pass out copies of *Time to Get Up!* Read the author's and illustrator's names. Ask children about the illustration on the cover.

▶ **What is the character in this picture doing?**

▶ **What do you think this book might be about?**

READ TOGETHER

Read the My Book with children, tracking the print as you read. Guide children to read along and to identify all the ways the little creature tries to wake his big friend.

PHONICS

Point to the books and the bed in the illustrations. Say the words *books* and *bed*, emphasizing the initial *b*— *b-b-books, b-b-bed*. Ask children to repeat the words.

▶ **What letter stands for the sound you hear at the beginning of the words?**

READ AND WRITE INDEPENDENTLY

Journal Invite children to read *Time to Get Up!* on their own or in small groups. Provide crayons and invite children to color the illustrations. Encourage children to have conversations with others about what they do when they get up in the morning.

HOME/SCHOOL CONNECTION Children can take home their My Book to share with family members and friends.

CENTER WORKSHOPS

Music & Movement

Do a *Dd* Dance

Play a game of musical *Dd*'s by placing the construction paper to make *Dd* stepping stones.

- Guide children in moving from stone to stone as the music is played.
- When the music stops, children can find a *Dd* stepping stone and call out something whose name begins with *Dd*. Allow children to use words that have been previously mentioned.
- Remove one stone each time the music stops.

Observation: How are children helping one another come up with *Dd* words?

MATERIALS

- Sheets of construction paper, each printed with *Dd*
- Crayons
- Lively music

Alphabet

In Search of *Dd*'s

Pair up "detectives" and send them in search of words with the letter *Dd*. Each pair will need a marker and index cards.

- Detectives may find things in the classroom whose names have the **/d/** sound at the beginning, middle, or end of the word.
- Ask one child to write on their cards the words for things that begin with *Dd* and the partner to circle the letter *Dd* in each word.
- Place the words in the pocket chart to be shared later with the whole group.

Observation: How do children show that they understand the relationship between the **/d/** sound and the letter *Dd*?

MATERIALS

- Index cards

DAY 10 OBJECTIVES

CHILDREN WILL:

- compare and contrast stories
- discuss problem solving in stories
- participate in writing a group chart
- identify rhyming words
- maintain /k/c and /d/d
- create a final project

MATERIALS

- *Caps for Sale*
- *Boots*
- *I Went Walking*
- *Carlos and the Squash Plant*
- Picture Cards for *Cc* and *Dd*

TECHNOLOGY

 Encourage children to use the drawing and writing tools in the **WiggleWorks Plus** Write area to complete the project and activities.

For more computer activities, see the Technology Teaching Plan.

Put It All Together

Sum It Up

COMPARE AND CONTRAST

Display the books children have read during the previous nine days. Discuss with children the main problem that the characters had in each of the books. Encourage children to share their questions or comments about each of the books.

ORAL LANGUAGE: DISCUSS PROBLEM SOLVING

Sing a song about problem solving, "The More We Solve Problems," to the tune of "The More We Get Together" to celebrate the end of the plan.

> ### The More We Solve Problems
> **The more we solve problems**
> **Solve problems, solve problems**
> **The more we solve problems**
> **The smarter (and happier) we'll be**

Present a problem-solving activity to children. Ask if they can make a paper bag fly. Give each child a bag to experiment with. Children may wad up their bags into balls, toss them, fold them, blow into them, or throw them. Encourage them to talk about the different ways they each solved the problem of making the bag fly.

Return to the books that are on display and remind children that each of the characters in the stories had to find a way to solve a problem. Discuss with children:

▶ **Which problem do you think was the hardest to solve? What made you feel that way?**

▶ **Have you ever had a problem like one that the characters in these books had? How did you solve it?**

▶ **Can you think of a problem you had that might make a good story?**

COMPARE AND CONTRAST CHART

Language Experience Chart

Display the books that the children have read during the previous nine days. Encourage children to recall and discuss the books. Respond to any questions they have.

- Make a language chart entitled, "We Try Different Ways to Solve Problems." Talk about the different problems in the books and how they were solved. Write children's responses on the language chart. Give children the opportunity to add their own pictures and writing to the chart. Display the chart as part of the documentation for what children have been doing.

MODIFY Instruction

EXTRA HELP

■ Guide children to understand problems and solutions by asking them about experiences in their daily life. Begin by suggesting that it is raining outside and the rain will make them wet. Ask, "What should I do to solve this problem?" Guide children to answer, "I should wear a raincoat or take an umbrella." **(GUIDED QUESTIONS)**

We Try Different Ways to Solve Problems

I Went Walking	Caps for Sale	Boots	Carlos and the Squash Plant
The girl sees a pig caked with dirt and washes it with a hose.	The peddler pulls off his own cap, throws it on the ground, and walks away.	The boy tries to put on his clothes before outdoor play is over.	Carlos takes a bath, and the plant growing from his ear disappears.

Observation:

How are children doing? Are they:
- comparing and contrasting stories and books?
- finding a variety of ways to solve problems?
- becoming comfortable doing their own form of writing?

MODIFY Instruction

EXTRA HELP

■ Help children distinguish between the /k/ and /d/ sounds by asking them to focus on the position of their mouth, lip, and tongue as they say each aloud. **(MODEL)**

PROFESSIONAL DEVELOPMENT

JOHN SHEFELBINE

What's the Difference Between Phonics and Phonological Awareness?

*Phonological awareness is the understanding that spoken words are made up of units of sound, the smallest of which is the phoneme. The word **not** has three phonemes—/n/, /o/, /t/. Phonics is the relationship between sounds in spoken words and how they are represented in print. So, phonics involves print, or sound-spelling relationships, while phonological awareness focuses on sounds.*

DAILY PHONICS

Maintenance

Ⓐ PHONOLOGICAL AWARENESS

Rhyme Word Match Invite children to play a matching game using the sets of picture cards below. Mix the cards in each set, and say each picture name. Have volunteers pick the two cards whose picture names rhyme. Tell them to repeat the name of each picture and then name another word that rhymes with the picture names.

bat, leaf, cat   rock, dog, sock

man, bus, pan   mop, top, pig

Ⓑ PHONICS ACTIVITY

Cats and Dogs Place the letter cards for *c* and *d* in a pocket chart. Then display the following picture cards: *cat, dog, cup, duck, coat.*

- Have children place the picture cards whose names begin with **/d/** under the *d* card, and the picture cards whose names begin with **/k/** under the *c* card.

- Encourage children to suggest other cards that could be added to each column of pictures or make their own pictures that can be added.

WEEKS 3 AND 4
PROJECT

Create a Storyboard

As children have engaged in reading stories about characters who try different ways of solving problems, they have discovered that there are a variety of ways to reach a solution. Now children can select a story from the last two weeks to dramatize with storyboards.

Reread the story children choose to refresh their thoughts about the details of the literature. If children select a rhyme, poem, or song from the *Big Book of Rhymes and Rhythms*, you may want to let children listen to the audiocassette in small groups.

Encourage children to retell the story selected. Talk about the sequence of events for the final project.

MATERIALS

- **Books and magazines that depict indoor and outdoor scenes**
- **Paper**
- **Pencils**
- **Clay**

BENCHMARKS

Monitor children's progress. Are they

- finding a variety of ways to solve problems?

- asking questions to reach solutions?

- Explain that a storyboard is a series of pictures that tell a story. Invite children to use paper and pencils to draw pictures for the storyboard.

- Provide magazines and books with photographs of indoor and outdoor scenes, and encourage children to use the photos for ideas.

- Children can work on their drawings independently. When the drawings are complete, work as a group to post the drawings in order.

- Provide clay and invite children to design the scenery. If children suggest other art materials to incorporate, provide these as needed. Suggestions are an excellent sign that children are finding different ways to solve problems!

 Take pictures for the class and individual portfolios.

WEEKS
5 AND 6

Kindergarten Goals
for Weeks 5 and 6

Oral Language/ Vocabulary

- participating in rhymes, songs, conversations, and discussions
- participating in choral reading
- exploring animal words, plant words, and number words
- exploring story vocabulary

Reading

- building alphabetic knowledge
- participating actively in shared reading
- engaging in emergent reading
- exploring concepts of print
- focusing on directionality: top to bottom
- reading riddles
- explore problem and solution
- using picture clues
- repetitive text
- reading high-frequency words

Writing

- writing about clay objects
- writing questions and answers
- writing letters: *Ee, Ff*
- making price tags and labels
- focusing on environmental print
- make a color chart
- writing a special name
- engaging in shared writing
- writing independently in Journals
- writing a language-experience chart

Listening/Speaking/ Viewing

- listening responsively to a read aloud
- identifying rhythm and rhyme
- developing phonological awareness
- retelling a story in their own words
- presenting dramatic interpretations of stories
- singing songs
- engaging in conversations
- relating personal experiences to literature
- comparing stories
- demonstrating visual literacy

Daily Phonics: *Ee* and *Ff*

- reciting classic poems, songs, and nursery rhymes
- naming and recognizing the letters
- recognizing sound/letter relationships
- generating words that begin with /e/, /f/
- decoding words using beginning sounds

Center Workshops and Project

- acquiring world knowledge through cross-curricular activities
- creating clay creations and inviting families to a celebration

WEEKS 5 AND 6
RESOURCES

Big Book

Meet the Author

Deborah Guarino wrote this book after seeing a "mama llama" at the zoo. It is her first book.

Meet the Illustrator

Steven Kellogg has illustrated over 80 popular books for children.

• **With Sentence Strips**

Available as audiocassette

Big Book of Rhymes and Rhythms

For teaching phonological awareness, the alphabet, and concepts of print.

• **"The Black Hen"**
• **"Five Little Fishies"**

Available as audiocassette

Read Aloud

Meet the Author/ Illustrator

Although Don Freeman and his wife lived in Santa Barbara, California, he always loved big cities. Don Freeman said of his work, "Creating picture books for children fulfills all my enthusiasms and interests and love of life."

Read Aloud

Meet the Reteller

Gerald McDermott has created numerous books and animated films for children. He is also the Primary Education Program Director for the Joseph Campbell Foundation on mythology in education.

ABC Book

Meet the Authors/ Illustrators

For many years, Bruce Johnson drew for the newspaper *The Montreal Star*. 250 of his drawings were published in the book *Montreal Souveniers*.

Side One

Side Two

SourceCard

• What do you see?
• Riddles

High-Frequency Reader

Storytelling

"The Three Billy Goats Gruff"

a Norwegian folk tale

My Read and Write Book

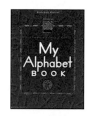

My Alphabet Book

ESL/ELD Teaching Guide

My Books

To take home to share.

WHERE DID THEY GO?

by Cass Hollander
Illustrated by Vincent Andriani

WHO CAN HELP?

by Cass Hollander
Illustrated by Mavis Smith

Introducing the Mentor

Becky Wible's job is to bring clay to life. To do it, she and the animators she works with have to ask questions, find answers, and try different solutions. It's a lot of work, but in the end they always solve the problem!

DAYS AT A GLANCE

WEEKS 5 AND 6

	Daily Phonics	Literature	Shared Writing	Workshops and Projects
DAY 1	Phonological Awareness: Oddity Task Review /b/b, /k/c, /d/d	***Apples, Alligators and also Alphabets*** by Odette and Bruce Johnson	Write About Clay Objects	Alphabet: Letters in the Sand Art: *Ee* Snakes
DAY 2	**Vowel /e/e** Phonological Awareness: Oral Segmentation: Syllables	***Is Your Mama a Llama?*** by Deborah Guarino illustrated by Steven Kellogg	Write Questions and Answers	Games: Animal Search Social Studies: Clay Creatures
DAY 3	**Vowel /e/e** Phonological Awareness: Alliteration Introduce Sound-Spelling	***Is Your Mama a Llama?*** by Deborah Guarino **High-Frequency Reader:** *Kittens*	Concepts of Print: Top-to-Bottom Write *Ee* Write Class Story	Science: Where Do the Animals Live? Art: Animal Scenes
DAY 4	**Vowel /e/e** Phonological Awareness: Rhyme Review Sound-Spelling	***Corduroy*** by Don Freeman	Make Price Tags and Labels	Art: Make a Stuffed Doll Math: A Bushel of Bears
DAY 5	**Vowel /e/e** Phonological Awareness: Rhyme Maintain Sound-Spelling	**"The Black Hen"** a rhyme ***Apples, Alligators and also Alphabets*** **My Book:** *Where Did They Go?*	Concepts of Print: Relate Speech to Written Word High-Frequency Words: *can, see, you*	Dramatic Play: Act Out *Ee*'s! Alphabet: Form Those *Ee*'s!

	Daily Phonics	Literature	Shared Writing	Workshops and Projects
DAY 6	Consonant /f/f Phonological Awareness: Alliteration	*The Three Billy Goats Gruff* retold by Margaret H. Lippert	Focus on Environmental Print	Dramatic Play: Story Sketch Art: Puppet Fun!
DAY 7	Consonant /f/f Phonological Awareness: Oddity Task Introduce Sound-Spelling	**SourceCard** What Do You See? Riddles **High-Frequency Reader:** *Kittens*	Make a Color Chart Write *Ff*	Art: Our Own *What Am I?* Science: Color My World
DAY 8	Consonant /f/f Phonological Awareness: Oral Blending Review Sound-Spelling	*Anansi the Spider: A Tale from the Ashanti* by Gerald McDermott READ ALOUD	Create a Special Name	Math: Shape Up! Games: Creepy Crawlers
DAY 9	Consonant /f/f Phonological Awareness: Rhyme Maintain Sound-Spelling	"Five Little Fishies" a rhyme *Anansi the Spider: A Tale from the Ashanti* **My Book:** *Who Can Help?*	Concepts of Print: Capital and Small Letters	Art: *Ff* Flags! Alphabet: Forming *Ff*
DAY 10	Consonant /f/f Phonological Awareness: Oral Segmentation: Beginning Sounds Phonics Maintenance	**Review Books from Weeks 5 and 6**	Make a Compare and Contrast Language Chart	Project: Clay Creations

Share the ABC Book

DAY 1 OBJECTIVES

CHILDREN WILL:

- orally blend and segment word parts
- review consonants /b/b, /k/c, /d/d
- make categories
- read *Apples, Alligators and also Alphabets*
- build alphabetic knowledge
- write a message
- explore story vocabulary
- engage in Center Workshops

MATERIALS

- *Apples, Alligators and also Alphabets*
- ABC cards
- Picture Cards, R33–34

GUIDED READING

To conclude each day's reading session, meet with guided reading groups. You might use Scholastic's Guided Reading Library or other books in your library.

DAILY PHONICS

Warm-Up: Wordplay

Ⓐ PHONOLOGICAL AWARENESS

Oral Segmentation: Beginning Sounds Invite children to play a guessing game. Tell them you are thinking of something in the room. Then give a clue and say the word, segmenting the beginning sound. For example: *It is something you throw. It is called a /b/. . . . all.* Continue a few times. Then invite children to give their own clues and segment the word.

Ⓑ PHONICS MAINTENANCE

Consonants /b/ b, /k/ c, /d/ d Show children the picture card for *bee* and ask them to name the animal. Encourage them to say the beginning sound—**/b/**—and name the letter that stands for that sound. Invite children to point to a *Bb* ABC Card. Continue in the same way with the *Cc* and *Dd* ABC Cards and the picture cards *cup* and *dog*.

Build Background

ORAL LANGUAGE: CATEGORIES

Have children look for animals and things that grow as you turn the pages of *Apples, Alligators and also Alphabets*. As children name items, list them on chart paper under the headings *Animals* and *Things That Grow*. Extend the activity by inviting children to name other objects found in the book. Help them think of categories for these objects.

PREVIEW AND PREDICT

Show the cover of *Apples, Alligators and also Alphabets* and ask children to name the letter that begins each word in the title. Review with children that the alphabet begins with the letters *a, b, c,* and *d*. Ask them what two letters come after *d?*

SET A PURPOSE

Ask children what other things they think will be in this book. Write down their ideas for *Ee* and *Ff* and invite them to listen to find out.

Read the ABC Book

ALPHABETIC KNOWLEDGE: *Ee* AND *Ff*

Read the ABC book, inviting children to join in as you say each letter's name. Pause on the *Ee* page of *Apples, Alligators and also Alphabets,* and help children identify the upper- and lowercase letters. Ask:

▶ **What animals did the authors use for the letter *Ee*? What else did they use in their illustration?**

Continue in the same way with the *Ff* page.

Respond to the Literature

TALK ABOUT IT

More About *Ee* and *Ff* Talk about the *Ff* page and review the names of the animals and objects whose names begin with *Ff*. Invite children to name other things that begin with *Ff*. Use these clues to help them:

▶ **It lives in the water. (fish)**

▶ **You have five of these on one hand. (finger)**

▶ **You use this to help you eat. (fork)**

Conclude by writing *E* and *F* on the chalkboard. Ask how the two letters are alike and how they are different.

THINK ABOUT IT

Focus on Letters Make a vertical list on chart paper of the letters of the alphabet. Ask a child to choose a page in the book, name the highlighted letter, and name the animals and objects on the page that begin with that letter. Write the responses next to the letter on the list. Invite children to name other objects they could add to the page. Then continue with other pages.

Apples, Alligators
and also Alphabets

MODIFY Instruction

GIFTED & TALENTED

☀ **Have children use masking tape to create a large uppercase *E* and a large lowercase *e* on the floor. Invite them to guide each other with their eyes closed as they "walk each letter." Can they figure out which is the letter *E* and which is the letter *e*? Repeat with *F* and *f*. (HANDS-ON LEARNING)**

ESL/ELD

▲ First, review the vocabulary with children, focusing on the more common words. Then play a riddle game. Provide descriptive clues about story vocabulary to help children make connections. For example, ask children to name an animal with a big trunk. **(ASSIST IN PROCESS)**

Shared Writing

WRITE ABOUT CLAY OBJECTS

Invite children to make a clay animal or object of their choice from *Apples, Alligators and also Alphabets*. Help them write a sentence about what they have made. Point out the word that names their clay animal or object and ask them to underline it. Encourage them to identify the first letter.

Designate an area where children's clay creations and sentences can be displayed. Invite children to look at the display and notice the underlined word that names each clay animal or object.

WRITE A MESSAGE

Children might enjoy writing a note to tell a classmate what they like about their clay creation.

Repeated Reading

EXPLORE STORY VOCABULARY

As you reread *Apples, Alligators and also Alphabets*, focus on unusual story words. Invite children to think about new vocabulary by asking questions such as:

▶ **Where would you find a harp? What does it sound like?**

▶ **Who has eaten quiche? What does it taste like?**

▶ **What kind of animal is a loon?**

You may also have children identify unusual animals and objects that are not mentioned in the text.

READ AND WRITE INDEPENDENTLY

Journal Place a copy of *Apples, Alligators and also Alphabets* in a quiet corner along with magnetic or cutout letters. Children can read the book and match the magnetic letters to each page. Invite children to practice writing the letters in their Journals. They might also write about their favorite illustration.

✓ Comprehension Check

ACT IT OUT

Invite children to work in groups of three or four to form the letter *E* with their bodies. Encourage them to speak courteously with other group members as they work. They may want to try it standing up or lying on a rug. How many ways can they form the letter? Repeat with the letter *F*.

CENTER WORKSHOPS

Letters in the Sand

Put a thin layer of sand in each tray. Display Alphabet Cards showing *Ee*. Model writing the letters in the sand with your finger. Encourage children to form *E* and *e* in the sand.

Invite children to form other letters and shapes in the sand.

Observation: Notice how children form the letters.

MATERIALS

- **Styrofoam trays**
- **Sand**
- **Alphabet card for *Ee***

Ee Snakes

Invite children to make clay snakes and then to manipulate them to form the letters *E* and *e*.

How can they change the letter *E* into an *e*?

You may wish to take photos of the children's work for documentation purposes and to share with family and friends.

Observation: Notice how children make their letters.

MATERIALS

- **Clay**
- **Plastic knives**
- **Alphabet Card for *Ee***

Share the Big Book

DAY 2 OBJECTIVES

CHILDREN WILL:

- clap syllables
- recognize /e/
- read and respond to *Is Your Mama a Llama?*
- recognize rhythm and rhyme
- write questions and answers
- review baby animal names
- recognize repetitive story structure
- engage in Center Workshops

MATERIALS

- *Is Your Mama a Llama?*
- Sentence Strips for *Is Your Mama a Llama?*
- My Read and Write Book, pp. 21–22

The Big Book is available on audiocassette in the Literacy Place Listening Center. The song is available on the **Sounds of Phonics** audiocassette.

DAILY PHONICS

Vowel /e/e

PHONOLOGICAL AWARENESS

Oral Segmentation: Syllables Sing "One Elephant Went Out to Play" to children. Sing it again, inviting children to sing along. Then say the word *elephant* and clap each syllable. Explain that each clap stands for one syllable. Ask children how many syllables are in the word *elephant*. Continue with *spider* and *enormous*.

Ask children what sound they hear at the beginning of the word *elephant*. Say the word *elephant,* isolating the beginning sound: *e-e-elephant*. Have children repeat.

> ### One Elephant Went Out to Play
> One elephant went out to play,
> Out on a spider's web one day.
> He had such enormous fun,
> He called for another elephant to come.

Build Background

ORAL LANGUAGE: ANIMAL BABIES

Show children a picture of a llama. (See the SourceCard.) Invite them to talk about what they know about how a llama looks and sounds. Explain that children will be reading about a baby llama. Ask children to think about baby animals that they have seen. Invite them to share words for animal babies.

PREVIEW AND PREDICT

Read the title *Is Your Mama a Llama?* as you point to each word. Which animal on the cover might be asking, *Is Your Mama a Llama?*

Read the Big Book

FOCUS ON RHYME AND RHYTHM

Encourage children to talk about what is happening in the illustrations on the half-title page, the title page, and the dedication page.

• Read the book, emphasizing the rhythm of the words.

• As you read, point out the pictures of the baby animals. Encourage children to predict the name of each baby animal's mama by using clues in the pictures and in the rhyming text.

Respond to the Literature

TALK ABOUT IT

Share Personal Responses Encourage children to share their personal responses to the animals in the book.

▶ How did Lloyd the Llama figure out who the mama was for each baby animal?

▶ Which animals in the book have you seen before? Where did you see them?

▶ Were you surprised when you found out about any of the animal mothers? Which ones?

THINK ABOUT IT

Chart Animal Names Review the names of animals and their babies that were discussed in the Build Background section. Discuss how animals often have different names as babies than as adults.

• Encourage children to share animal baby and adult names they are familiar with.

• Write the names on a chart like the one shown. Show photos if available.

• Add the names of the baby and adult animals in the book to the chart, leaving room for children to add illustrations and photographs.

Baby Name	Adult Name
Kitten	Cat
Kid	Goat
Joey	Kangaroo

Is Your Mama a Llama?

PROFESSIONAL DEVELOPMENT

ADRIA KLEIN

Developing Oral Language Through Read Alouds

Oral language is a cornerstone of the primary curriculum. Throughout the day children should be engaged in activities that help them explore concepts and create meaning by talking to you and fellow classmates. In addition, extend children's oral language skills through read alouds that are rich in language and conceptual knowledge. Read alouds are a great vehicle for expanding a child's vocabulary and knowledge of the world.

OBSERVATION

How are children doing? Are they:

- using pictures clues and other clues to predict text?
- recognizing the repetitive structure of the story?
- recalling story events?

Keep the answers to these questions in mind when planning Day 3, Revisit the Big Book.

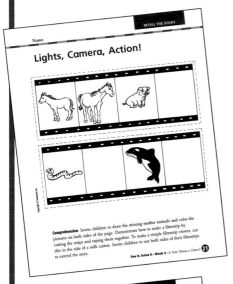

Comprehension Invite children to draw the missing mother animals and color the pictures on both sides of the page. Demonstrate how to make a filmstrip by cutting the strips and taping them together. To make a simple filmstrip viewer, cut slits in the side of a milk carton. Invite children to use both sides of their filmstrips to extend the story.

See It, Solve It • Week 5 • *Is Your Mama a Llama?* **21**

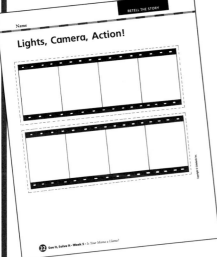

See It, Solve It • Week 5 • *Is Your Mama a Llama?* **22**

My Read and Write Book, pp. 21–22

Shared Writing

WRITE QUESTIONS AND ANSWERS

Display the first few Sentence Strips for *Is Your Mama a Llama?* Read the title on the first Sentence Strip and ask children how they can tell the sentence is a question. Let them point out the question mark. Remind them that this question-and-answer format continues throughout the story. Continue reading aloud the Sentence Strips and have children raise their hands each time you read a question.

> Is Your Mama a Llama?

> "Is your mama a llama?" I asked my friend Dave.

> "No, she is not," is the answer Dave gave.

Next, write at the top of chart paper, "My mama's a _____." Read it with children, and ask volunteers to write or copy animal names from the story to finish the sentence. Invite children to illustrate the chart.

Repeated Reading

MAKE PREDICTIONS

Show children the cover of *Is Your Mama a Llama?* and guide them to read the title along with you. As you reread the book, invite children to point out and recite the question "Is your mama a llama?" each time it appears.

Encourage children to predict the name of each animal's mama before you turn the page. After turning the page, invite children to point to the adult animal's name.

READ AND WRITE INDEPENDENTLY

Journal Place copies of *Is Your Mama a Llama?* in the Reading Center for children to read on their own or in small groups. Provide the audiocassette so children can listen to the story as they read. Children can draw pictures of the animal characters and label them in their Journals.

✓ Comprehension Check

ACT IT OUT

Encourage children to act out *Is Your Mama a Llama?* You can be the narrator, reading each page, while children take turns being Lloyd and his animal friends. Encourage children to speak with appropriate volume when acting out the story.

CENTER WORKSHOPS

Animal Search

Make copies of the Animal Sorting Cards and invite children to play "Find Your Animal Family."

Each child picks an Animal Sorting Card. Explain to children that they can move around the room, pretending to be the animals on the cards they chose. Then they try to find the child who picked the same animal. When they think they have found their partner, they ask a question like Lloyd asked in the book, such as "Is your mama a duck?" or "Is your mama a cow?"

Observation: How do children pretend to be the different animals?

MATERIALS

- Animal Sorting Cards

Clay Creatures

Add some new tools to the claymaker's studio, such as a garlic press and clay hammer. Show children how to push clay through the press so that it oozes out like curly animal fur. Encourage children to explore using this and the new tools.

Children can have fun making clay sculptures of animals from *Is Your Mama a Llama?* and of other animals they know. Encourage children to label their creations.

Observation: Notice how children explore the new tools.

MATERIALS

- *Is Your Mama a Llama?*
- Clay
- Garlic press
- Plastic knives
- Rolling pins
- Clay hammer

DAY 3 OBJECTIVES

CHILDREN WILL:

- listen for alliteration
- recognize and write /e/e
- reread *Is Your Mama a Llama?*
- understand directionality
- participate in a choral reading
- read the High-Frequency Reader: *Kittens*
- engage in Center Workshops

MATERIALS

- *Is Your Mama a Llama?*
- High-Frequency Reader: *Kittens*
- My Alphabet Book, p. 7
- My Read and Write Book, pp. 23–24

The Big Book is available on audiocassette in the Literacy Place Listening Center.

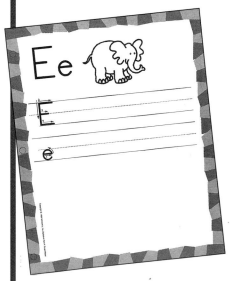

My Alphabet Book, p. 7

Revisit the Big Book

and Read the High-Frequency Reader

DAILY PHONICS

Vowel /e/e

A PHONOLOGICAL AWARENESS

Alliteration Say the following alliterative sentence, emphasizing the /e/ sound.

Evan and Ed had eggs.

Ask children to repeat it. Say each word again slowly. Ask children to pretend they are breaking an egg every time they hear /e/ in the sentence.

B CONNECT SOUND-SPELLING

Introduce Vowel /e/e On the chalkboard write *Evan and Ed had* **eggs.** Point out to children that the letter *e* stands for /e/ at the beginning of *egg, Ed,* and *Evan.*

- Ask children to say the sound /e/ with you.
- Repeat *Evan, Ed,* and *eggs* and ask children to exaggerate the /e/ sound in each name.

Letter Formation

WRITE THE LETTER

Write *Ee* on the chalkboard. Point out the capital and small forms of the letter. Model how to write the letter using the rhymes provided.

- Have children write both forms of the letter in the air with their fingers.
- When writing the letters, help children use the correct pencil grip and guide them to position their paper correctly.

E	e
Down *(Pull down straight.)* **Let your pencil glide.** **Then three little lines** **go out to the side.** *(Make three short lines out to the right.)*	**Make a short line this way.** *(Make short horizontal line.)* **Then start a circle** **Go over the top.** *(Pull up and around.)* **And just before it closes up,** **Stop, stop, stop.**

Reread the Big Book

OPTIONS

Choral Reading Encourage children to read the line "Is your mama a llama?" each time it appears in the story. Provide a prompt, such as holding up a finger, to help children follow along.

Animal Illustrations Pause when you get to each illustration that shows a baby animal with its mother. Ask children to look at the picture carefully and guide them to use words that compare the baby animal to the adult animal.

▶ **Is the baby bigger or smaller than the adult?**

▶ **Does the baby have longer or shorter hair/legs than the adult?**

Rhyming Words Pause after you read a passage with rhyming words and invite children to identify the words that rhyme. As children become familiar with the rhyme scheme, replace the rhyming words with others that are obviously incorrect. Encourage children to correct you when they hear the error.

READ AND WRITE INDEPENDENTLY

Journal Place copies of *Is Your Mama a Llama?* in the Reading Center for children to read alone or in small groups. Children can write in their Journals about their favorite animal baby and adult in the book.

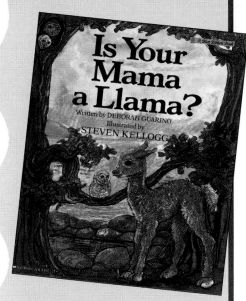

Is Your Mama a Llama?

MODIFY Instruction

ESL/ELD

▲ Go over each illustration showing the mother and baby animal. Have English language learners practice saying the names of all the pictured animals. **(PICTURE CLUES)**

Concepts of Print

DIRECTIONALITY: TOP-TO-BOTTOM

Display *Is Your Mama a Llama?* Use a pointer to track the print as you read aloud. When you reach the end of a line, have a child point to the beginning of the next line to show where you should read next.

• When you come to a page with text above and below the art, point out that you start reading at the top of the page.

• Continue explaining that you look at the picture when you come to it, and then read the text below the picture.

• Invite volunteers to track print as you continue reading.

My Read and Write Book, p. 23

Kittens

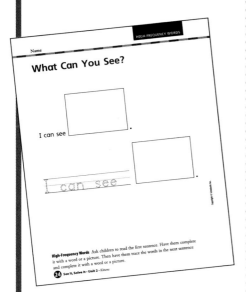

**My Read and Write Book,
p. 24**

Read High-Frequency Reader

**INTRODUCE
THE BOOK**

Show the book *Kittens*. Read the title and the author's name. Explain that the book tells about a boy's pets.

▶ **Do you have a pet? What kind?**

▶ **What kind of pets do you think will be in the story?**

**HIGH-
FREQUENCY
WORDS: *you***

Write the sentence stem *Can you see* _____ on the board and read it. Review the words *can* and *see.* Have volunteers find them on the Word Wall. Then underline the word *you* and write it on a note card. Read it aloud.

• Display the card and have children read the word.

• Help children spell it aloud, clapping on each letter.

• Ask children to write in the air as they state aloud each letter.

Invite children to complete the sentence stem by naming something they can see. Write each new sentence on the board and have children read it aloud.

**SHARE THE
HIGH-
FREQUENCY
READER**

Read the story aloud, tracking the print. Invite children to point to the high-frequency words *can, you, I,* and *see.*

• After each page, ask children to answer the question, count the kittens, and tell where they see them.

• The story also reviews consonant /k/c. Help children use their knowledge of this sound-spelling to decode words.

**SHARED
WRITING**

Invite children to write a class story called *Can you see?*

• Ask children to choose a pet or other animal they would like to write about.

• Then have volunteers read each page of *Kittens* aloud, substituting the name of the new animal for *kitten* or *kittens*.

• Write the new sentences on chart paper, leaving room under each for a small illustration.

CENTER WORKSHOPS

Science

MATERIALS

- Yarn
- Glue
- Pictures of animals from *Is Your Mama a Llama?*
- Animal Sorting Cards

Where Do the Animals Live?

The animals in *Is Your Mama a Llama?* live in different homes. Some live on land, others live in or on water. Invite children to browse through their Little Book to see where the llama, the bat, the swan, the cow, and other animals live.

Use yarn to form two large circles on the floor. Use an index card to label one circle "land" and the other "water." Let children place the animal pictures in the appropriate circle. They will soon realize that some animals, such as seals and swans, live on land and on water.

Observation: Notice how children discover that some animals live on both land and water. How do they share this information?

Art

Animal Scenes

Let children work together to design a diorama filled with different kinds of clay animals. They may want to set up a zoo, a farm, or a variety of animal habitats.

Suggest that children use the paper and markers to draw a background and label their creations.

Observation: How do children use the clay to create animal environments?

MATERIALS

- Shoebox
- Clay
- Rolling pin
- Drawing paper
- Scissors
- Markers

DAY 4 OBJECTIVES

CHILDREN WILL:

- recognize rhyming words
- review vowel /e/*e*
- read and respond to *Corduroy*
- explore story problems and solutions
- respond to literature
- write labels and price tags
- recognize repetitive language
- engage in Center Workshops

MATERIALS

- *Corduroy*
- My Read and Write Book, p. 25

Share the Read Aloud

DAILY PHONICS

Vowel /e/*e*

A PHONOLOGICAL AWARENESS

Rhyme Read aloud the rhyme below. As you reread it, pause after the second, third, and fourth lines and ask children which word rhymes with *Gwen*. Help children notice the /e/ sound in each rhyming word.

> This is a poem about Gwen.
> She was a very smart hen.
> She could write her name with a pen.
> And count all the way up to ten.

B CONNECT SOUND-SPELLING

Crack an Egg Have children pretend they are cracking an egg, walking with an egg on their heads, or doing other things with an egg. Then write the word ***egg*** on the board, read it aloud, and circle the letter *e*. Remind children that the letter *e* stands for /e/.

Build Background

ORAL LANGUAGE: STORES

Ask children if they have ever been to a department store or other large store. Invite them to talk about it. Where did they go? What did they see there? Did the store have more than one floor? How many floors? How did they get from one floor to another?

PREVIEW AND PREDICT

Show the cover of *Corduroy* and the read the title and the author/illustrator's name. Ask:

▶ **What is corduroy?**

▶ **What do you think this book is about?**

SET A PURPOSE

Ask children why they think this book is called *Corduroy*. Draw their attention to the bear on the cover and have them predict what is going to happen to the bear.

Share the Read Aloud

FOCUS ON PROBLEMS/ SOLUTIONS

As you read the story aloud, ask children to listen for the problems that Corduroy and the girl have. After each problem is identified, invite children to predict how it will be solved. Ask children to listen to find out. After reading, talk about how the characters' problems were solved.

▶ How did Corduroy get a button?

▶ How did Lisa get her very own bear?

Corduroy

Respond to the Literature

TALK ABOUT IT

Share Personal Responses Encourage children to share how they would feel in a large department store at night. Children may also enjoy telling about their own stuffed animals and other toys.

▶ **How do you think Corduroy might be feeling as he wanders through the store looking for his button?**

▶ **Why did Corduroy want to find his button?**

▶ **If you were Corduroy, where would you look for the button?**

THINK ABOUT IT

Tell the Girl's Story This story tells about a night in Corduroy's life. Ask children to think about how the little girl spent the same night.

▶ **How do you think the girl felt when she left the store without Corduroy?**

▶ **What do you think she talked about with her mother that night?**

▶ **How do you think the girl felt when she took Corduroy home with her?**

MODIFY Instruction

ESL/ELD

▲ Children acquiring English may need additional practice talking about stores and shopping. Invite children to draw a picture of a store in their neighborhood, showing the different items for sale. Encourage children to talk about the store and the items pictured. **(MAKE CONNECTIONS)**

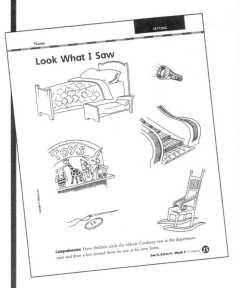

My Read and Write Book, p. 25

Shared Writing

MAKE PRICE TAGS AND LABELS

Invite children to imagine that their classroom is a department store and that everything in the store is for sale.

- Have children identify the "merchandise" and make a label for each item with an index card.
- Encourage them to write the letters that they know on the labels. Let children decide how many cents each item will cost.
- Help them write the number with a cent sign for each price tag. Children can attach the labels to the merchandise and set up a pretend store.

WRITE A NOTE

Encourage children to write a short note inviting a classmate to shop at the pretend store.

Repeated Reading

CHIME IN ON REPETITION

As you reread the story, ask children to chime in every time Corduroy says he has always wanted something. Each time ask what Corduroy always wanted and make a list of responses on the chalkboard. At the end of the story ask: How many times does Corduroy say "I've always wanted..."?

READ AND WRITE INDEPENDENTLY

Journal Place *Corduroy* in the Reading Center so that children can read it independently or in small groups. Children may want to draw pictures of and label their own stuffed animal or other special toy in their Journals.

✓ Comprehension Check

RETELL THE STORY

Invite volunteers to retell the story as you show the pictures in the book. On each page encourage children to tell what Corduroy is doing and how he is probably feeling.

CENTER WORKSHOPS

Make a Stuffed Doll

Children can work together in groups to make a stuffed doll, each group making a different part.

Distribute the clothing and other material that each group will need for its part of the doll. Guide children to stuff each piece; then staple it yourself.

- stuff the socks; staple them to the pant legs.
- stuff the pants; staple them to the bottom of the shirt.
- stuff the gloves; staple them to the shirt's sleeves.
- stuff the shirt and the paper bag; staple bag to the neck of shirt.
- decorate the head and body with collage materials.

Observation: How do children make their stuffed dolls unique?

MATERIALS

- **Paper bag**
- **Child-size shirt**
- **Pants, gloves, socks**
- **Newspapers**
- **Glue, stapler**
- **Collage material**

A Bushel of Bears

Invite children to bring old teddy bears or other stuffed animals to school. Children can categorize their bears by color, length, weight, age, or some other category.

- Invite children to set up their own teddy bear store, encouraging them to display the bears in a variety of ways. Provide paper for price tags, signs, or bear names. Children can also count the number of bears collected, and display the total for everyone to see.
- Use the bears for counting eyes, legs, arms, and for any teddy bear games.

Observation: What are children's favorite ways to display the bears?

MATERIALS

- **Old stuffed animals**
- **Ropes**
- **Tape measures**
- **Pan balance**
- **Magnifiers**
- **Paper**
- **Pencils**
- **Crayons or markers**

Sounds and Letters

DAY 5 OBJECTIVES

CHILDREN WILL:

- recognize rhyming words
- recognize /e/e
- connect spoken words to written words
- review high-frequency words
- read My Book: *Where Did They Go?*
- engage in Center Workshops

MATERIALS

- *Big Book of Rhymes and Rhythms*, p. 10
- Sentence Strips for "The Black Hen"
- *Apples, Alligators and also Alphabets*
- My Book: *Where Did They Go?*
- My Read and Write Book, p. 26

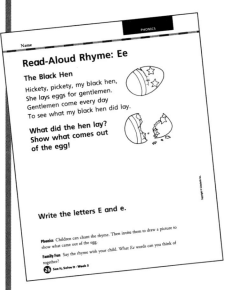

My Read and Write Book, p. 26

For additional practice see *Scholastic Phonics K*, pp. 31–34. Also see Sound and Letter Book: *Ed Likes Eggs.*

DAILY PHONICS

Vowel /e/e

A **PHONOLOGICAL AWARENESS**

Rhyme Read aloud the rhyme "The Black Hen" from *the Big Book of Rhymes and Rhythms*. Ask children what sound they hear at the beginning of the words *eggs* and *every*. Invite children to repeat the words, emphasizing the beginning sound—/e/.

Have children repeat the rhyme with you. Invite them to notice the words that rhyme with *hen* and *day*.

Big Book of Rhymes and Rhythms, p. 10

B **CONCEPTS OF PRINT**

Place the *Big Book of Rhymes and Rhythms,* the Sentence Strips for "The Black Hen," and a pocket chart in the Reading Center.

- Read "The Black Hen," asking volunteers to place the appropriate Sentence Strip in the pocket chart as you read each line.
- Invite volunteers to frame each word in a sentence with their fingers.
- Then have children point to the words that begin with the letter *e.*

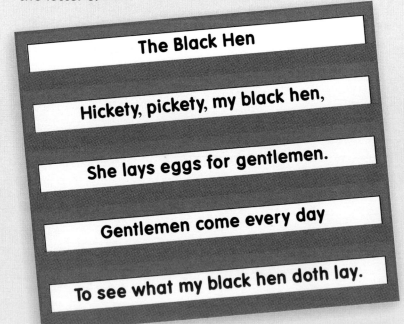

© CONNECT SOUND-SPELLING

Alphabetic Principle Remind children that the letter *e* stands for **/e/** as in *eggs*. Open *Apples, Alligators and also Alphabets* to the *Ee* page and have children find the elves and elks in the picture. Ask children the name of the other animal in the picture that begins with **/e/.** Then invite them to make up a sentence about the things in the picture.

Model from the Literature Open *Is Your Mama a Llama?* to the last page and show children the word *END*. Point out the capital *E* at the beginning of the word. Together, read the words *THE END*. Point out that all the letters are capitals. Tell children that the author may have done this to make the words look important.

ABC Book Explain to children that they are going to make a new page for their own ABC book. Have children suggest animals, objects, and people whose names begin with **/e/.** When the list is complete, invite children to work together to create an *Ee* page for their ABC books.

① VOCABULARY: HIGH-FREQUENCY WORDS

Write the incomplete sentence *Can you _____ ?* on the chalkboard. Then do the following:

- Review the two high-frequency words. If necessary, review the read-spell-write routine for each word.

- Have a volunteer act out something he or she can do. For example, bend.

- Write the action word in the sentence and have the child read the question. Invite the rest of the class to "answer" by doing the action.

- Continue with another action from a different volunteer.

EXTRA HELP

■ Reinforce **/e/e** by placing on the table pictures of animals and objects whose names begin with the letter *e* and the sound **/e/** such as *elephant, elk, elf, elbow,* and *egg.* Label the animals and objects. Encourage children to talk about them using the words on the labels. **(USE PICTURES)**

TECHNOLOGY

 Guide children to write the groups of letters shown on the **WiggleWorks Plus** Magnet Board, leaving a space in front of each group. Ask them to place the letter *e* in front of each group of letters and to read the new words. Offer children clues such as: *something to eat for breakfast; not the beginning but the _____.*

 The rhyme in the *Big Book of Rhymes and Rhythms* is available on the **Sounds of Phonics** audiocassette.

Where Did They Go?

Read My Book

INTRODUCE THE BOOK

Let children know they are going to get their own book that they can read on their own and take home.

▶ **What are some animal homes called?**

▶ **Have you ever seen a bird in a nest or a squirrel in a tree? What did these homes look like?**

PREVIEW AND PREDICT

Pass out copies of *Where Did They Go?* Read the title and the author's and illustrator's names. Ask children about the illustration on the cover.

▶ **What animal is this?**

▶ **Where do you think it's going?**

▶ **What do you think this book might be about?**

READ TOGETHER

Read the My Book with children, tracking the print as you read. Guide children to read along in their copies and to point out where each animal goes.

PHONICS

Ask children to say the word *did* aloud.

▶ **What letter stands for the sound you hear at the beginning of the word?**

Have children find the word in the book.

READ AND WRITE INDEPENDENTLY

Journal Encourage children to read *Where Did They Go?* on their own or in small groups. Provide crayons and invite children to color the illustrations.

HOME/SCHOOL CONNECTION

Children can take home their My Book to share with family members and friends.

CENTER WORKSHOPS

Act Out *Ee's!*

Help children make up a skit about an engineer who drives an engine with an elephant and elves riding in it. Invite them to make props to use in dramatic play. For example, they might make an elephant trunk and ears, an engineer's cap and whistle, and elf costumes.

Have children choose the parts they will play and act out the skit. Children may want to recite the familiar rhyme "Engine, Engine, Number Nine." Write the words on a chart and let children decorate it to enliven the area.

Observation: How do children act out words that begin with *Ee?*

MATERIALS

- Chart paper
- Marker
- A variety of arts and crafts materials

Form Those *Ee's!*

Display Alphabet Card *Ee* to model the forms for *E* and *e*.

Invite children to form the letters *E* and *e* in the sand.

Encourage children to experiment with forming the letters *E* and *e* by rolling tubes of clay and placing them together to form the letters.

Let children make the letters *E* and *e* with finger paint in paint trays or on finger paint paper.

Observation: Which children particularly like forming letters?

MATERIALS

- Sand
- Alphabet Card *Ee*
- Clay
- Trays
- Finger paints
- Finger paint paper

DAY 6 OBJECTIVES

CHILDREN WILL:

- listen for alliteration
- recognize /f/f
- listen to *The Three Billy Goats Gruff*
- discuss problem solving
- sequence story events
- make signs
- recognize characters' feelings
- engage in Center Workshops

MATERIALS

- Chart paper
- Markers
- Tape recorder

GUIDED READING

To conclude each day's reading session, meet with guided reading groups. You might use Scholastic's Guided Reading Library or other books in your library.

Storytelling Circle

DAILY PHONICS

Consonant /f/f

PHONOLOGICAL AWARENESS

Alliteration Read aloud the title "A Fly and a Flea in a Flue." Say aloud the words *fly*, *flea*, and *flue*, isolating the /f/ sound: *f-f-fly, f-f-flea, f-f-flue*. Ask children to repeat.

- Explain that authors often use many words in a sentence that begin with the same sound to make the reading and listening more fun.

- Recite the poem asking children to listen for, and clap when they hear, words beginning with /f/ as in **fan.**

A Fly and a Flea in a Flue

A fly and a flea in a flue
Were imprisoned, so what could they do?
Said the fly, "Let us flee!"
"Let us fly!" said the flea.
And they flew through a flaw in the flue.

READ
Aloud

The Three Billy Goats Gruff

A Norwegian folk tale
retold by Margaret H. Lippert

Once upon a time there were three billy goats. They were brothers, and their last name was Gruff.

They lived by the side of a river. Across the river was a pasture of sweet green grass. There was a bridge across the river, but the billy goats had never crossed the bridge.

Under the bridge lived an ugly troll. He had eyes as big as saucers and a nose as long as a poker.

Build Background

ORAL LANGUAGE: EVERYDAY PROBLEMS

Encourage children to talk about the different kinds of problems that people have everyday.

▶ **What problem have you had? How did you solve it? Who helps you solve problems?**

Tell the Story

LISTEN FOR SEQUENCE

Explain that in Scandinavian folklore, a troll is a giant or dwarf who lives underground or in a cave.

As you read, encourage children to listen for the sequence of story events. After the littlest billy goat crosses the bridge, ask the following questions:

▶ **Do you think a bigger billy goat is really going to cross the bridge? What do you think will happen when he does?**

Respond to the Literature

TALK ABOUT IT

Share Personal Responses Encourage children to participate in a conversation about the story.

▶ **How did the littlest and middle-sized billy goats Gruff get away from the troll?**

▶ **Do you think it was a good idea to tell the troll what they did? Why or why not?**

MODIFY Instruction

ESL/ELD

▲ Use visuals as a strategy to activate children's prior knowledge and build background. After drawing the troll and the goats, ask children if they know of another story with similar characters. Mention *The Three Little Pigs.* Encourage them to describe these stories, such as "The Three Little Pigs" and make connections to *The Three Billy Goats Gruff.* **(MAKE CONNECTIONS)**

One day, the littlest billy goat decided to cross the bridge. "Trip, trap, trip, trap," went his hoofs on the bridge.

"WHO'S THAT GOING OVER MY BRIDGE?" roared the troll.

"It is only I, the littlest billy goat Gruff," said the small billy goat, in his very small voice.

"I'm coming to eat you up," said the troll.

The littlest billy goat thought quickly. "Oh, don't do that," he said. "My brother is coming after me. He is bigger than I am."

"A bigger billy goat is a bigger meal," said the troll. "Be off with you!" So the littlest billy goat went across the bridge. He began to eat the sweet green grass.

Then the middle-sized billy goat decided to cross the bridge.

"Trip, trap, trip, trap," went his hoofs on the bridge.

"WHO'S THAT GOING OVER MY BRIDGE?" roared the troll.

"It is only I, the middle-sized billy goat Gruff," said the billy goat. His voice was louder than his brother's.

"I'm coming to eat you up," said the troll.

"Don't do that," said the middle-sized billy goat. "My brother is coming after me. He is even bigger than I am."

"A bigger billy goat is a bigger meal," said the troll. "Be off with you!" So the middle-sized

THINK ABOUT IT

Discuss Story Problems Ask children to consider both sides of the story problem.

▶ **Who, besides the billy goats, had a problem?**

▶ **Why didn't the troll want anyone walking on his bridge?**

Shared Writing

FOCUS ON ENVIRON-MENTAL PRINT

Invite children to think of a sign that the troll could place on his bridge, such as "Keep Off!" Help children make a sign to place on a bridge that they make in the Block Center.

Retell the Story

RECOGNIZE CHARACTERS' FEELINGS

As you retell the story, pause occasionally and ask children to tell how the characters might feel.

▶ **How do you think the little billy goat Gruff feels when he hears the troll's loud voice?**

▶ **How do you think the troll feels when he hears that a bigger billy goat is coming?**

 **Comprehension Check**

ACT IT OUT

Help children form groups of four to reenact the story.

For narration, tape-record the story in your own voice or allow children to retell it.

READ Aloud

continued from page T127

billy goat went across the bridge to eat sweet grass with his brother.

Then up came the big billy goat. "TRIP TRAP, TRIP TRAP," went his hoofs on the bridge.

"WHO'S THAT GOING OVER MY BRIDGE?" roared the troll.

"IT IS I, THE BIG BILLY GOAT GRUFF," said the big billy goat. His voice was almost as loud as the troll's.

"I'm coming to eat you up," said the troll.

"Come on," said the big billy goat. "I'm not afraid of you." The troll climbed onto the bridge. But the big billy goat was ready. First he trampled the troll with his hard hoofs. Then he butted the troll into the river. That was the end of the troll.

Then the big billy goat went over the bridge to eat grass with his brothers. They all got so fat they could hardly walk home again.

So snip, snap, snout,
This tale's told out!

CENTER WORKSHOPS

Story Sketch

Set up the Dramatic Play Center so that children can enjoy acting out the story again and again.

The characterization may be enhanced by simple props that children find or create themselves. For example, they could use a towel or rug for a bridge, fingers for horns, or strips of yarn taped to their chins for beards.

Observation: Do children perform the story in sequence?

MATERIALS

- Simple props

Puppet Fun!

Provide paper plates and various art materials. Invite children to decorate the paper plates to portray characters from the story. They can use objects such as pipe cleaners for horns and buttons for eyes.

- Attach the plates to tongue depressors or craft sticks so that children can hold their puppets.

- Encourage children to have fun using their puppets.

Observation: How do children use the various art materials to create their puppets?

MATERIALS

- Paper plates
- Paints
- Crayons
- Buttons
- Plastic bottle tops
- Fabric swatches
- Craft sticks or tongue depressors
- Pipe cleaners

DAY 7 OBJECTIVES

CHILDREN WILL:

- identify words with the same beginning sound
- recognize and write consonant **/f/f**
- solve riddles
- explore colors
- write a group chart
- reread the High-Frequency Reader: *Kittens*
- read sentences with numbers
- engage in Center Workshops

MATERIALS

- *Problem Solving*, SourceCard 3
- *Is Your Mama a Llama?*
- High-Frequency Reader: *Kittens*
- Sentence Strips for *Kittens*
- My Alphabet Book, p. 8
- Picture Cards, R33–34

My Alphabet Book, p. 8

Read the SourceCard

DAILY PHONICS

Consonant /f/f

A PHONOLOGICAL AWARENESS

Oddity Task: Beginning Sounds Explain to children that you will be showing them three picture cards. Have them say the name of each picture and choose the two that begin with the same sound. Make additional picture cards for the following words: *feet, five, fork, fire, fox.*

- **fan, fork, coat**
- **fox, fire, lip**
- **fish, feet, bee**
- **five, moon, fox**

B CONNECT SOUND-SPELLING

Introduce Consonant /f/f Page through *Apples, Alligators and also Alphabets* until you get to the **Ff** page. Point out that the letter **f** stands for **/f/** as in **feet**.

- Ask children to say the sound **/f/** with you.
- Say the names of items in the illustration and ask children to exaggerate **/f/** at the beginning of each name.

Letter Formation

WRITE THE LETTER

Write **Ff** on the chalkboard. Point out the capital and small forms of the letter. Model how to write each form, using the rhymes below.

- Invite children to write both forms of the letter in the air with their fingers. Ask children to make the letter's sound as they practice writing.

F	f
Down, down, down, *(Pull straight down.)* **Across once,** *(Pull across left to right.)* **Across twice,** *(Pull across left to right.)* **'Til you reach town.**	**Writing an f Is no hard riddle.** *(Curve up, to the left, and then straight down.)* **It's an upside-down hook With a line through the middle.** *(Add horizontal line across the middle.)*

Share the SourceCard

Side One

SIDE ONE

Look at Llamas Guide children to look at the photograph. Read aloud the question, "What do you see?"

▶ **What animal do you see in the picture?**

▶ **What else do you see? What colors are in this picture?**

Invite children to talk about things they see in the photograph. Encourage them to use color names in their descriptions. Invite children to compare the llamas in the photograph with the llama in *Is Your Mama a Llama?*

Side Two

SIDE TWO

Read the Riddles Read the riddles on side two of the SourceCard. Volunteers can suggest answers to the riddles. Then read the answers.

▶ **What makes these riddles funny?**

▶ **What do you notice that is the same about these riddles?**

Point out the question-and-answer pattern. Ask children to point to the question marks. Read the riddles aloud again and let children chime in with the answers.

Shared Writing

MAKE A COLOR CHART

Have children name the colors in the rainbow on the SourceCard (side two). Provide markers in those colors.

• Invite children to use the marker of the corresponding color to write the rainbow colors on a chart.

• Have children name objects in the classroom that have the same colors.

• Add the names of these objects to the chart with the marker of the corresponding color. Invite children to draw the objects with the markers.

Kittens

EXTRA HELP

■ To reinforce one-to-one correspondence of numbers 1 through 5, write each numeral on an index card. Invite children who need extra help to draw a card, name the numeral, and then display that number using math manipulatives. **(HANDS-ON LEARNING)**

Revisit High-Frequency Reader

REREAD THE BOOK

Invite children to join you as you reread *Kittens*.

On the first page, have children review the three high-frequency words *can, you,* and *see.* Explain how the pictures and their knowledge of sound-spellings can help them read the last two words in the sentence.

DECODING STRATEGIES

- As you go through the book, point to each word, the initial letter, any other sound-spellings children have learned, and the picture clue, pausing long enough for children to read before you do.

- Model blending words, as needed. For example, have children use their knowledge of /k/c to decode *can.*

CONCEPTS OF PRINT: SENTENCES

Show the sentence strip for page one. Point out how the sentence begins with a capital letter and ends with a question mark. Invite a volunteer to point to the first word and the question mark. Continue with other pages.

ORAL LANGUAGE: NUMBERS

Point out the numerals on each page of the book. Have children name each numeral and count the kittens shown. On chart paper, write the numbers *1* through *5* in a column. Recite them with children. Then ask children to draw kittens or other pets to represent each number.

READ FOR FLUENCY

Give each child a copy of *Kittens.*

- Invite children to read with a partner and take turns reading the pages and counting the kittens.

READ AND WRITE INDEPENDENTLY

Journal Place copies of the High-Frequency Reader in the Reading Center. Children can draw or write in their Journals about how many *toys, desks, teachers,* and *chalkboards* they see. Provide the sentence stem, *I can see _____ .*

HOME/SCHOOL CONNECTION

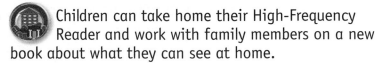

Children can take home their High-Frequency Reader and work with family members on a new book about what they can see at home.

CENTER WORKSHOPS

Our Own *What Am I?*

Show the book *What Am I?* and ask children to tell how they could make their own version. Children can cut a shape from the center of a sheet of paper. Then, on another sheet of paper, they can draw and color a large picture or cut and paste a picture from a magazine.

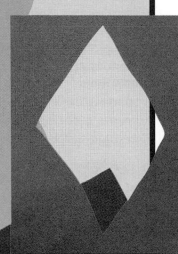

- Help children staple or tape the paper with the cutout window on top of the one with the picture. Make sure a portion of the picture shows through the window.

- Help children write short clues about what is behind the window. Display the pages for the entire class to enjoy or staple them together to create a class book.

Observation: Notice the kinds of clues children create.

MATERIALS

- *What Am I?* (from Week 1)
- Construction paper
- Coloring materials
- Scissors
- Tape

Color My World

Let children conduct experiments with color.

- Make colored lenses by cutting a piece of colored cellophane the size of a paper plate. Cut out matching circles in the centers of two paper plates. Staple the two plates together with the cellophane sandwiched between them. Make several of these lenses, using different colors. Invite children to look through one lens at a time and then try overlapping combinations of lenses.

- Guide children to lightly brush watercolor paint over paper and notice how the colors mix together.

Observation: How do children work together to complete their science experiments?

MATERIALS

- Colored cellophane
- Paper plates
- Scissors
- Stapler
- Watercolor paints
- Cups of clear water
- Paper
- Paintbrushes

CHILDREN WILL:

- orally blend words
- review /f/f
- read and respond to *Anansi the Spider*
- use picture clues
- explore story problems and solutions
- reenact the story
- create a special name
- engage in Center Workshops

MATERIALS

- *Anansi the Spider: A Tale from the Ashanti*
- *My Read and Write Book,* p. 27

Share the Read Aloud

DAILY PHONICS

Consonant /f/f

A PHONOLOGICAL AWARENESS

Oral Blending Say the following word parts aloud. Have children blend them. Provide modeling as needed.

/f/ . . . un	/f/ . . . eet	/f/ . . . ish
/f/ . . . an	/f/ . . . ive	/f/ . . . ix

B CONNECT SOUND-SPELLING

Is It Fun? Write the word *fun* on the chalkboard. Circle the letter *f* and remind children that this letter stands for /f/. Invite children to name other words that begin with /f/. Write each word on the chalkboard and have volunteers circle the letter *f*. Review the words and have children decide which name something fun.

Build Background

ORAL LANGUAGE: TALENTS

Tell children that the story tells about the different talents of Anansi the spider's seven sons. Invite children to talk about something they think they are good at.

Explain that Anansi is a folk hero of the Ashanti people of Ghana. Point out Ghana on a map. Share the background information on Africa in the book's prologue.

PREVIEW AND PREDICT

Have children look at the cover. Read the title and the author/illustrator's name.

▶ **What do you think the design on the cover is?**

▶ **What do you think the story is about?**

SET A PURPOSE

Ask children to predict what talents Anansi's sons will have. Write ideas on chart paper. Encourage children to listen as you read to find out if their predictions are correct.

~~~~~~

Share the Read Aloud

USING PICTURE CLUES

Encourage children to listen to the story and guide them to look at how the pictures show the special ability of each of Anansi's sons. Take time to explore unfamiliar concepts with children, such as what See Trouble is able to do or what Game Skinner can do.

• When you come to the picture of all six sons at the beginning of the book, ask children how they can tell the difference between the spiders. Discuss the different design on each spider.

Anansi the Spider

~~~~~~

Respond to the Literature

TALK ABOUT IT

Share Personal Responses Ask children if they liked the story. Encourage them to tell which parts of the story were most interesting. Let children describe events in their own words.

▶ **Which picture do you like best?**

Invite children to talk about class events where they worked together to solve a problem.

SING ABOUT IT

Sing a Song Children might enjoy singing "The Eensy, Weensy Spider." After singing, encourage children to discuss the eensy, weensy spider's problem and how it was solved.

THINK ABOUT IT

Talk About Story Ending Invite children to talk about the ending of the story, after Anansi has been saved.

▶ **What was the prize for saving Anansi?**

▶ **Which son do you think should get the prize? Why?**

▶ **Why did Anansi make the decision he did?**

▶ **What was the globe of light?**

▶ **Do you think Nyame's decision was a good one? Why or why not?**

Let children reenact the argument that Anansi and his sons had near the end of the story. Children can make and wear picture cards in the dramatization to represent the sons.

MODIFY Instruction

EXTRA HELP

■ As you read the story, pause often to summarize the major points. Children may listen more attentively if the story is being summarized by a puppet that acts as your reading assistant. (SUMMARIZE)

My Read and Write Book, p. 27

Shared Writing

CREATE A SPECIAL NAME

Encourage children to recall each son's name and his special talent. Then invite children to create names for themselves that reflect a talent they have.

• Have children make a name tag by writing the letters for the sounds they know in the name. They can draw a picture or a design to illustrate the name.

• Children can wear their name tags around their necks, displaying their talents just as the designs on Anansi's sons show their skills.

Repeated Reading

PROBLEMS AND SOLUTIONS

As you reread the story, pause to discuss each situation that Anansi encounters. Ask children to recall which son will help solve the problem. Make a chart showing each problem and how the son helped solve it.

ILLUSTRATOR'S CRAFT

Explain how the pictures are drawn in the traditional style of the Ashanti people. Point out that the Ashanti people use simple shapes in their art. Ask children to look at the picture of the spider on the first story page. Have them point out the simple shapes of the spider's body, eyes, mouth, nose, and legs. Then ask children to find simple shapes in other story illustrations.

READ AND WRITE INDEPENDENTLY

Journal Place *Anansi the Spider* in the Reading Center so children can read it on their own. Children can create new illustrations and story episodes about Anansi and his sons in their Journals.

✓ Comprehension Check

ACT IT OUT

Invite children to reenact the story with spider puppets. They can create spider puppets by inserting eight short pipe cleaners into a Styrofoam ball and then decorating it with markers. Children who show a special interest in this dramatic play might enjoy telling the story themselves or performing their puppet play for a larger audience.

CENTER WORKSHOPS

Shape Up!

Invite children to use paper shapes to create animal pictures in the style of the book illustrations. Suggest that they arrange the paper shapes on construction paper before gluing them in place.

- Children may want to cut out their own shapes from construction paper and create backgrounds of trees, clouds, and buildings.

Observation: How do children use the shapes to make the animals and other objects?

MATERIALS

- Precut shapes of various sizes and colors
- Scissors
- Construction paper
- Glue

Creepy Crawlers

Invite children to trace one of their hands onto a piece of paper.

- Explain that spiders have eight legs. You might have the children count the legs on a spider in one of the story illustrations.

- Ask children to count the "legs" on their paper. Do they know how many more legs to add to make eight? After they have eight legs on their spiders, they can draw faces and add decoration.

Observation: Do children notice the variation in the eight legs of the spiders?

MATERIALS

- Crayons or markers
- Paper

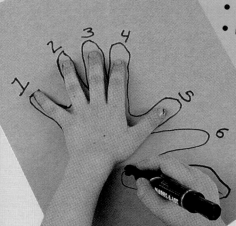

DAY 9 OBJECTIVES

CHILDREN WILL:

- listen for /f/
- recognize sound-spelling relationship for /f/*f*
- connect spoken and written words
- review high-frequency words
- read My Book: *Who Can Help?*
- engage in Center Workshops

MATERIALS

- *Big Book of Rhymes and Rhythms,* p. 11
- **Sentence Strips for "Five Little Fishies"**
- *Apples, Alligators and also Alphabets*
- *Is Your Mama a Llama?*
- **My Book:** *Who Can Help?*
- **My Read and Write Book, p. 28**

My Read and Write Book, p. 28

For additional practice see *Scholastic Phonics K,* pp. 35–38. Also see Sound and Letter Book: *Four Furry Feet.*

Sounds and Letters

Consonant /f/f

A **PHONOLOGICAL AWARENESS**

Rhyme Read aloud "Five Little Fishies" from the *Big Book of Rhymes and Rhythms.* Ask children what sound they hear at the beginning of the words **five** and **fishies.** Invite children to join you as you reread the poem. Emphasize the beginning sound of words that start with **/f/.**

On a third reading, encourage children to notice the rhyming word pairs.

Big Book of Rhymes and Rhythms, p. 11

B **CONCEPTS OF PRINT**

Place the *Big Book of Rhymes and Rhythms,* the Sentence Strips for "Five Little Fishies," and a pocket chart in the Reading Center.

- Read "Five Little Fishies," asking children to hold up another finger each time a new fish speaks.
- Reread the rhyme together. Ask volunteers to place the appropriate Sentence Strip in the pocket chart after each line is read.
- Then invite children to point to words with the letter **F** or **f.** Read aloud each word they find. Then have children frame the letter **F** or **f** and tell if it is a small or capital letter.

Five little fishies swimming in a pool.

First one said, "The pool is cool."

Second one said, "The pool is deep."

Third one said, "I want to sleep."

ESL/ELD

▲ To reinforce words that begin with *Ff,* set up a box filled with items that begin with /f/, such as *felt, fuzz,* and *feathers.* Invite children to feel the objects and guess what they are, using the model *It feels like* _____. Then label each object. **(MULTISENSORY TECHNIQUES)**

Ⓒ CONNECT SOUND-SPELLING

Alphabetic Principle Remind children that the letter *f* stands for **/f/** as in *fan.* Page through *Apples, Alligators and also Alphabets* as children chant the letters. Stop on the letter *Ff.* Read the sentence on the page and have children find the *flies, fleas,* and *furry feet* in the illustration. Invite them to make up silly sentences about *flies, fleas,* or *furry feet.*

Ff as in Feet Distribute Little Books of *Is Your Mama a Llama?* and invite children to look for words that begin with *Ff.* Help children read the words they find. Invite them to look through the book for illustrations of the *Ff* words. For example, when children point to the word *feet* on the third story page, they might point to the bat's feet in the illustration on the following page.

ABC Book Explain to children that they are going to make a new page for their own ABC book. Have children suggest animals, objects, and people whose names begin with **/f/.** When the list is complete, invite children to work together to create the *Ff* page for their ABC books.

Ⓓ VOCABULARY: HIGH-FREQUENCY WORDS

Display a picture of a beach, park, or other scene. Write the incomplete sentence **Can you see a _____ ?** on the board.

- Review each high-frequency word in the sentence. If necessary, review the read-spell-write routine.
- Invite children to complete the sentence stem by naming something they can see in the picture. Write each new sentence on the board and invite a volunteer to read the new sentence.
- Have classmates answer the question by pointing to the object in the picture.

TECHNOLOGY

 Invite children to write *fix* on the **WiggleWorks Plus** Magnet Board. Ask them to copy it and then replace the *i* with *o.* Ask what word this makes. Repeat with the other word pairs shown.

The rhyme in the *Big Book of Rhymes and Rhythms* is available on the **Sounds of Phonics** audiocassette.

WHO CAN HELP?

by Cass Hollander
Illustrated by Mavis Smith

SCHOLASTIC

Who Can Help?

MODIFY Instruction

EXTRA HELP

■ To reinforce understanding, invite children to act out the story as you read it aloud. **(ACT IT OUT)**

Read My Book

INTRODUCE THE BOOK

Let children know that they are going to get their own book that they can read on their own and take home.

Talk with children about the ways that the characters in the books you read helped one another solve problems.

▶ **How do you feel when you have a problem?**

▶ **Do you usually try to solve it yourself or do you ask for help?**

PREVIEW AND PREDICT

Pass out copies of *Who Can Help?* Read the author's and illustrator's names. Talk about the cover illustration.

▶ **What do you think these people are going to do?**

▶ **What do you think this book might be about?**

READ TOGETHER

Read the My Book with children, tracking the print as you read. Guide children to read along in their copies and to notice how the girl tries to be like her brother.

PHONICS

Ask children to say the word *dig* aloud.

▶ **What letter stands for the sound you hear at the beginning of the word?**

Help children find the word in their books.

READ AND WRITE INDEPENDENTLY

Journal Encourage children to read *Who Can Help?* on their own or in small groups. Provide crayons and invite children to color the illustrations.

HOME/SCHOOL CONNECTION

Children can take home their My Book to share with family members and friends. Suggest that children involve other family members or friends in a game or project.

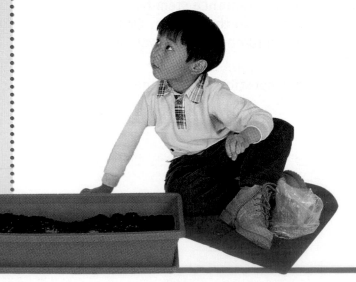

CENTER WORKSHOPS

Ff Flags!

Invite children to make **Ff** flags to hang around the room. Guide children to find **Ff** words for their flags in picture dictionaries and ABC books.

Children may discover that there are a number of farming and plant words that begin with **Ff**, such as *field, farm, flower, fern, feed,* and *fence.* Encourage children to draw pictures on their flags.

Observation: How do children go about finding words that begin with **Ff** to put on their flags?

MATERIALS
- **Construction paper**
- **Markers**

MATERIALS
- **ABC Card: Ff**
- **Clay**

Forming *Ff!*

Display ABC Cards to model the forms of **F** and *f.* Invite children to create clay coils or snakes and place them together to form the letters.

When children have successfully created the letters, encourage them to form objects with names that begin with **Ff** and label them with the letter.

Observation: How do children use the models when forming **Ff?**

DAY 10

DAY 10 OBJECTIVES

CHILDREN WILL:

- compare and contrast the books they've shared
- participate in writing a group chart
- maintain /e/e, /f/f
- create a final project

MATERIALS

- *Is Your Mama a Llama?*
- *Corduroy*
- *Anansi the Spider*

TECHNOLOGY

 Encourage children to use the drawing and writing tools in the **WiggleWorks Plus** Write area to complete the project and activities.

Put It All Together

Sum It Up

FOCUS ON SOLVING PROBLEMS

Engage children in a conversation about the problem-solving activities they have participated in together during the unit. Encourage them to talk about how to see problems, use clues, ask questions, and solve problems.

ORAL LANGUAGE: SONG

Sing the song "London Bridge Is Falling Down" as an example of problem solving.

London Bridge Is Falling Down

London Bridge is falling down,
Falling down, falling down.

London Bridge is falling down,
My fair lady.

Build it up with iron bars,
Iron bars, iron bars.

Build it up with iron bars,
My fair lady.

Build it up with gold and silver,
Gold and silver, gold and silver.

Build it up with gold and silver,
My fair lady.

Encourage children to identify the problem presented.

- Can they offer solutions to save London Bridge?

Add to the text or replace it with additional verses, traditional or made-up, such as "Build it up with wood and clay" or "Wood and clay will wash away." Singers may also enjoy acting out each verse of the song.

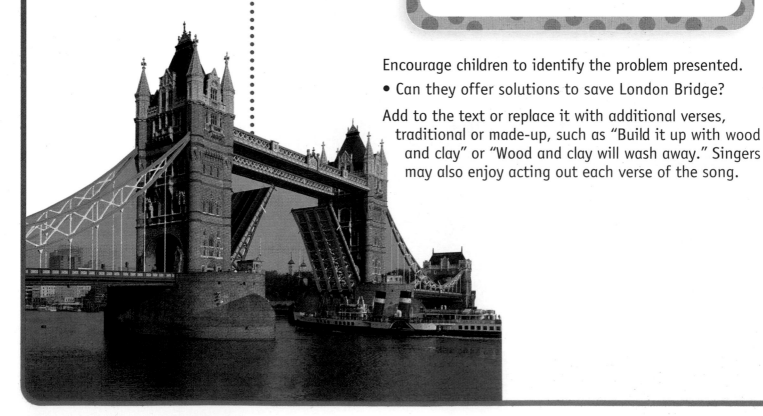

Language Experience Chart

COMPARE AND CONTRAST CHART

Display and revisit *Corduroy, Anansi the Spider,* and *Is Your Mama a Llama?* Encourage children to talk about the problems and solutions in each book. Work with children to chart out each problem and solution.

- Create a class book of problems. Invite each child to create a page for the book by drawing a picture of one of the story characters engaged in solving a problem. Encourage children to write about what they drew.

MODIFY Instruction

GIFTED & TALENTED

✳ Divide the class into small groups and encourage children to act out the problems and solutions of each story. This will give them the opportunity to detect details they might have missed during the discussion. **(ACT IT OUT)**

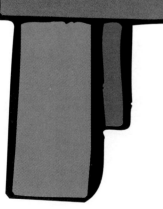

We Solve Problems

Is Your Mama a Llama?	Corduroy	Anansi the Spider
Problem: The baby llama doesn't know who its mother is.	Problem: lost his button	Problem: how to help Anansi
Solution: Baby llama asks questions.	Solution: looks for clues	Solution: working together

Observation:

How are children doing? Are they:
- using a variety of approaches to solve problems?
- finding clues and asking questions?
- comparing and contrasting the characters' problems?

TEACHER TIP

To help children understand that different sounds are made in different ways, choose two contrasting sounds such as /d/ and /f/. Ask children what position their tongue and lips are in when making these sounds. Suggest that they watch your mouth as you make each sound. Then have them feel whether or not a burst of air is made when they make each sound.

MODIFY Instruction

ESL/ELD

▲ Help children distinguish between the /e/ and /f/ sounds by modeling the position of mouth, lips, and tongue for each sound and having children copy you. Point out that the /f/ sound is made by putting your top teeth on your bottom lip. **(MODEL)**

Maintenance

Ⓐ PHONOLOGICAL AWARENESS

Four Funny Fish Read aloud the following phrase: *four funny fish*. Have children repeat the words. Then ask them to say the sound they hear at the beginning of each word—**/f/.** Help children to think of other words that begin with /f/ to replace *fish*. For example: *four funny faces, four funny foxes.*

Continue by helping children replace *fish* with words that begin with /e/. For example: *four funny elves, four funny eggs*. Review the /e/ sound.

Ⓑ PHONICS ACTIVITY

Funny Bulletin Board Display the phrases *four funny fish* on one side of a bulletin board and *four funny eggs* on the other side of the bulletin board.

• Read the words aloud as you point to each one. Then have children read them with you.

• Have volunteers point to the letter at the beginning of each word and say the sound it stands for.

• Invite children to draw a picture of *four funny fish* or *four funny eggs*.

• Help children label their drawings.

• Display children's drawings on the corresponding side of the bulletin board.

WEEKS 5 AND 6
PROJECT

Clay Creations

Throughout the unit, children shared books and stories concerning Problem Solving. At the end of weeks 2 and 4, children selected a story for dramatization with clay and storyboards. Center Workshops have incorporated constructing characters and making props. Now children are ready to create dioramas and share all their work with their families and friends.

MATERIALS

- **Shoeboxes**
- **Clay**
- **Paints**
- **Paper**
- **Markers**
- **Collage materials**
- **Glue**

BENCHMARKS

Monitor children's progress. Are they

- gaining meaning from print and pictures?

- becoming problem solvers?

- beginning to express opinions and offer suggestions?

Work with children to select a story you have read in the last two weeks.

- Divide the class into small groups. Work with children to decide which scene each group will create as a diorama.

- Provide each group with a shoebox, clay, and paints. Children can work together using clay to create characters and other objects from the scene. They can decorate with paint and collage materials.

Invite family members, school personnel, and friends to the special display of clay creations and other projects children have worked on during the Problem Solving unit. Display the books children have read and the charts they have written.

Be sure to take pictures during this celebration to add to the class portfolio and provide documentation of children's work.

TEACHER RESOURCES
BIBLIOGRAPHY

Books for Sharing

✳ Cultural Connection   ★ Kid Picks   ✖ Science   🌐 Social Studies   ▦ Math   🎭 The Arts

WEEKS 1 AND 2

Brown Bear, Brown Bear, What Do You See?
by *Bill Martin, Jr.*
illustrated by *Eric Carle*
Henry Holt & Co., 1983 ★ ✖
A variety of animals tell what they see in this colorful classic.

Have You Seen Birds?
by *Joanne Oppenheim*
illustrated by *Barbara Reid*
Scholastic, Inc., 1988 ✖
This engaging book introduces birds by asking readers which they have seen.

Have You Seen My Duckling?
by *Nancy Tafuri*
Greenwillow Books, 1984 ★ ✖
A mother duck searches for a missing duckling in this engaging Caldecott Honor Book.

Somebody and the Three Blairs
by *Marilyn Tolhurst*
illustrated by *Simone Abel*
Orchard Books, 1991 ★ 🎭
This funny book reverses the familiar situation of "The Three Bears."

The Three Billy Goats Gruff
by *Paul Galdone*
Clarion Books, 1981 ✳ 🌐
Galdone enjoyably retells another classic folk tale.

Will I Have a Friend?
by *Miriam Cohen*
illustrated by *Lillian Hoban*
Aladdin, 1989 ★ 🌐
Paul's first-day-of-school anxieties are forgotten when he makes a new friend.

WEEKS 3 AND 4

Harold's ABC
by *Crockett Johnson*
HarperCollins, 1963 ★ 🎭
Harold draws the alphabet and gets himself into and out of problems.

I Have a Sister—My Sister Is Deaf
by *Jeanne Whitehouse Peterson*
illustrated by *Deborah Ray*
HarperCollins, 1977 ✳ 🌐
A girl describes how her younger sister, who is deaf, uses her other senses to play piano and do many other things.

The Jacket I Wear in the Snow
by *Shirley Neitzel*
illustrated by *Nancy Winslow Parker*
Scholastic Inc., 1992 ★ ▦ ✖
A catchy rhyme chronicles the accumulation of the many layers of a girl's winter clothing.

No Milk!
by *Jennifer Ericsson*
illustrated by *Ora Eitan*
Tambourine Books, 1993 ★ ✖
A boy tries many ways to get milk from a cow.

The Trek
by *Ann Jonas*
Greenwillow Books, 1985 ✳ ▦
Two girls turn a walk into an adventure.

WEEKS 5 AND 6

Arrow to the Sun: A Pueblo Indian Tale
by *Gerald McDermott*
Viking Press, 1974 ✳ 🎭
The artist won a Caldecott Medal for this retelling of a Pueblo myth.

It Could Always Be Worse: A Yiddish Folk Tale
by *Harve, Kaethe, and Margot Zemach*
illustrated by *Margo Zemach*
Farrar, Straus & Giroux, 1977 ✳ 🌐
In this retelling of a classic folk tale, a villager discovers an unusual solution to a noisy household.

Mouse Count
by *Ellen Stoll Walsh*
Harcourt Brace Jovanovich Inc., 1991 ★ ▦
Ten mice outwit a greedy snake in a story that doubles as a counting book.

Nick Joins In
by *Joe Lasker*
Albert Whitman & Co., 1980 🌐
Nick, in his wheelchair, goes to school and finds that he has a role to play, too.

Red Dancing Shoes
by *Denise L. Patrick*
illustrated by *James Ransome*
Tambourine Books, 1993 ✳
An African-American girl must find a way to repair her shoes.

Who Wants One?
by *Mary Serforzo*
illustrated by *Keiko Narahashi*
McElderry Books, 1989 ✳ ▦
A girl counts with her younger brother from one to ten.

Books With Phonic Elements

Amanda and April
by *Bonnie Pryor*
illustrated by *Diane de Groat*
William Morrow & Co., Inc., 1986
Two sisters share adventures on the way to Violet's birthday party. (A)

Bear's Bargain
by *Frank Asch*
Scholastic Inc., 1992
Bear and Little Bird help each other make their wishes come true. (B)

Cookie's Week
by *Cindy Ward*
illustrated by *Tomie dePaola*
Putnam, 1988
Follow Cookie, a cat, for a week of his adventures. (C)

Dad's Dinosaur Day
by *Diane Dawson Hearn*
Macmillan Publishing Co., 1993
Mikey and his dad have fun when his dad pretends to be a dinosaur. (D)

An Extraordinary Egg
by *Leo Lionni*
Alfred A. Knopf, Inc., 1994
Three frogs befriend the creature that hatches from an enormous egg. (E)

Four Famished Foxes and Fosdyke
by *Pamela Duncan Edwards*
illustrated by *Henry Cole*
HarperCollins, 1995
Four foxes fail to filch fowl, but find other food in this funny book. (F)

Books in Other Languages

Spanish

Cuenta ratones
by Ellen Stoll Walsh
Fonda de Cultura Economica,
1992 ★ 🎴
Ten mice outwit a greedy
snake in this counting book.

**¿De quién es este
sombrero?**
by Cecilia Avalos
illustrated by
Mary Lynn Blasutta
Scholastic Inc., 1993 🌐
Readers guess a person's oc-
cupation from his or her hat.

Flecha al sol
by Gerald McDermott
Viking Press, 1991 ✳ 🌐
The artist won a Caldecott
Medal for this retelling of a
Pueblo myth.

¿Tu mamá es una llama?
by Deborah Guarino
illustrated by Steven Kellogg
Scholastic Inc., 1992
★ 🦋
A baby llama seeks another
animal with a llama for a
mother.

Chinese

Caps for Sale
by Esphyr Slobodkina
Shen's, 1982 ✳ ★
In this Chinese-language
version, monkeys take caps
from a peddler.

The Mouse Bride
by Monica Chang
illustrated by Lesley Liu
Shen's, 1992 ✳
In this bilingual
Chinese/English book,
father mouse searches for
a husband for his daughter.

Japanese

**Brown Bear, Brown Bear,
What Do You See?**
by Bill Martin, Jr.
illustrated by Eric Carle
Multicultural Distributing
Center, 1983 ★ 🦋
In this Japanese translation,
a variety of animals tell what
they see.

Illustrator Study:
Leo and Diane Dillon

**Why Mosquitoes Buzz in
People's Ears**
by Verna Aardema
Scholastic Inc., 1987
A mosquito tells a tale that
creates a chain reaction.

Northern Lullaby
by Nancy White Carlstrom
Putnam, 1992
Art and text evoke the
Northern night sky in this
beautiful book.

Switch on the Night
by Ray Bradbury
Alfred A. Knopf, Inc., 1993
A boy finds comfort in
nighttime.

Teacher's Bookshelf

**All I Really Need to Know I
Learned in Kindergarten**
by Robert Fulghum
Ivy Books, 1993
This wise and funny book
presents the basic principles
of kindergarten.

**The Delany Sisters' Book of
Everyday Wisdom**
by Sara and A. Elizabeth
Delany With Amy Hill Heath
Kodansha International, 1994
With over a century of living,
these African-American
women pass on some of their
observations about life.

Paula
by Isabel Allende
HarperCollins, 1995
This Latin-American novelist
wrote a moving family history for her invalid daughter.

Sophie's World
by Jostein Gaarder
Farrar, Straus & Giroux, Inc.,
1994
A bestseller in Europe, this
mystery novel unfolds with
questions sent to the main
character.

Technology

For more information about Scholastic's technology, call 1-800-SCHOLASTIC

Software

WiggleWorks Plus
Scholastic (Win/Mac)
This CD-ROM component for
Kindergarten through Grade 2 of
Literacy Place supports children's
language development. Its activi-
ties integrate reading, writing,
listening, and speaking.

I Spy
Scholastic (Win/Mac)
These scavenger-hunt games
build reading, math, problem-
solving, and logic skills.

Scholastic Reading Counts!
(Formerly "The Electronic Bookshelf") This
reading motivation/management program is
for students at all reading levels.

Usborne's Animated First Thousand Words
Usborne/Scholastic (Win/Mac)
This vocabulary tool introduces pre- and be-
ginning readers to English and Spanish words.

**Huggly's Sleepover:
I'm Ready for Kindergarten**
Scholastic (Win/Mac)
The first software with a complete balance of
essential skills for Kindergarten.

Internet

www.scholasticnetwork.com
This comprehensive online curriculum service
for grades K–8 features unit-by-unit extensions for Literacy Place.

www.scholastic.com
Scholastic's corporate web site includes Literacy Place resources and unit-related Internet links.

Other Sites
The Internet is growing and changing every
day, so be sure to preview all sites before
your students visit them.

READING	GRADE	K	1	2	3	4	5
Print Awareness							
recognize that print messages represent spoken language and conveys meaning		●	●				
knows print moves left-right, top-bottom		●	●				
understands that written words are separated by spaces		●	●				
know the difference between individual letters and words		●	●				
know the difference between capital and lower-case letters		●	●				
know the order of the alphabet		●	●				
recognize conventions of capitalization and punctuation		●	●				
understand that spoken words are represented in written language by specific sequences of letters		●	●				
recognize parts of a book		●	●	●	●	●	●
recognize that there are correct spellings		●	●	●	●	●	●
recognize distinguishing features of paragraphs				●	●	●	●
Phonological Awareness							
divide sentences into individual words		●	●	●			
identify, segment, and combine syllables		●	●	●	●		
produce and distinguish rhyming words from non-rhyming		●	●	●	●		
identify and isolate initial and final sounds		●	●	●	●		
blend sounds		●	●	●	●		
segment one-syllable words into individual phonemes clearly producing beginning, medial, and final sounds		●	●	●	●		
Letter-Sound Relationships							
name and identify each letter of the alphabet		●	●				
understand that written words are composed of letters that represent sounds		●	●				
learn and apply letter-sound correspondences of:							
consonants (beginning, middle, end)		●	●	●			
short vowel sounds		●	●	●			
phonograms/word families/patterns		●	●	●			
digraphs			●	●	●	●	●
blends			●	●	●	●	●
long vowel sounds			●	●	●	●	●
diphthongs			●	●	●	●	●
variant vowels			●	●	●	●	●
blend initial letter-sounds with common vowel spelling patterns to read words		●	●	●	●		
decode by using all letter-sound correspondences within regularly spelled words		●	●	●	●	●	●
use letter-sound knowledge to read decodable texts		●	●	●	●		

● = direct instruction   ▓ = mastery

	GRADE	K	1	2	3	4	5
Word Identification							
decode by using all letter-sound correspondences within a word		●	●	●	●	●	●
use common spelling patterns to read words		●	●	●	●	●	●
use structural cues to recognize compounds, base words, and inflectional endings			●	●	●	●	●
use structural cues to recognize prefixes and suffixes				●	●	●	●
use root words and other structural cues to recognize derivational endings				●	●	●	●
identify multisyllabic words by using common syllable patterns				●	●	●	●
recognize high-frequency irregular words		●	●	●	●	●	●
use knowledge or syntax and context to support word identification and confirm meaning		●	●	●	●	●	●
read regular and irregular words automatically			●	●	●	●	●
locate meanings, pronunciations, and derivations of unfamiliar words using dictionaries, glossaries, and other sources			●	●	●	●	●
Fluency							
read regularly in independent-level materials			●	●	●	●	●
read regularly in instructional-level materials			●	●	●	●	●
read orally from familiar texts			●	●	●	●	●
self-select independent-level materials			●	●	●	●	●
read silently for increasing amounts of time			●	●	●	●	●
demonstrate characteristics of fluent and effective reading			●	●	●	●	●
adjust reading rate based on purpose			●	●	●	●	●
read aloud			●	●	●	●	●
Text Structures/Literary Concepts							
distinguish different forms of texts		●	●	●	●	●	●
understand simple story structure		●	●	●	●	●	●
distinguish fiction from nonfiction		●	●	●	●	●	●
distinguish fact from fantasy		●	●	●	●	●	●
distinguish among types of text		●	●	●	●	●	●
distinguish between roles of the author and illustrator		●	●	●	●	●	●
identify text as narrative or expository				●	●	●	●
compare communication in different forms		●	●	●	●	●	●
understand and identify literary terms		●	●	●	●	●	●
analyze characters		●	●	●	●	●	●
identify importance of setting		●	●	●	●	●	●
recognize and analyze story problem/plot and resolution		●	●	●	●	●	●
judge internal consistency or logic of stories and texts			●	●	●	●	●
recognize that authors organize information in specific ways			●	●	●	●	●

GRADE	K	1	2	3	4	5
identify purposes of different types of texts	●	●	●	●	●	●
recognize the distinguishing features of genres		●	●	●	●	●
describe the author's perspective or point of view			●	●	●	●
Variety of Texts						
read fiction, nonfiction, and poetry for pleasure and information	●	●	●	●	●	●
use graphs, charts, signs, captions and other informational texts to acquire information	●	●	●	●	●	●
read classic and contemporary works	●	●	●	●	●	●
read from print a variety of genres for pleasure and information	●	●	●	●	●	●
read from electronic sources a variety of genres for pleasure and information	●	●	●	●	●	●
read to accomplish various purposes		●	●	●	●	●
select varied sources, i.e., nonfiction, novels, textbooks, newspapers and magazines for information and pleasure		●	●	●	●	●
read for varied purposes, i.e., to be informed, entertained, appreciate writer's craft, and discover models for writing		●	●	●	●	●
Vocabulary Development						
discuss meanings and develop vocabulary through meaningful/concrete experiences	●	●	●	●	●	●
develop vocabulary by listening and discussing selections read aloud	●	●	●	●	●	●
identify words that name persons, places or things, and actions	●	●	●	●	●	●
use dictionaries, glossaries, technology, and context to build word meanings and confirm pronunciation		●	●	●	●	●
demonstrate knowledge of synonyms, antonyms and multiple-meaning words		●	●	●	●	●
draw on experiences to bring meanings to words in context		●	●	●	●	●
use thesaurus, synonym finder, dictionary and software to clarify meanings and usage				●	●	●
determining meanings of derivatives by applying knowledge of root words and affixes			●	●	●	●
use curricular content areas and current events to study words			●	●	●	●
Comprehension						
use prior knowledge and experiences	●	●	●	●	●	●
establish purposes for reading	●	●	●	●	●	●
retell or act out the order of events in stories	●	●	●	●	●	●
monitor own comprehension		●	●	●	●	●
draw, discuss, and describe visual and mental images		●	●	●	●	●
make and explain inferences, i.e., determining important ideas, causes and effects, making predictions, and drawing conclusions		●	●	●	●	●
identify similarities and differences in topics, characters, problems, and themes	●	●	●	●	●	●
produce summaries of text selections		●	●	●	●	●
represent text information through story maps, graphs, charts, outline, time line, or graphic organizer	●	●	●	●	●	●

● = direct instruction   ▢ = mastery

GRADE	K	1	2	3	4	5
distinguish fact from opinion			●	●	●	●
practice different kinds of questions and tasks, including test-like questions		●	●	●	●	●
use cause and effect, or chronology to locate and recall information		●	●	●	●	●
determine main idea and supporting details	●	●	●	●	●	●
paraphrase and summarize text	●	●	●	●	●	●
draw inferences and support with text evidence and experience		●	●	●	●	●
find similarities and differences across texts in treatment, scope, organization		●	●	●	●	●
answer different types and levels of questions, i.e., open-ended, literal, and interpretative; multiple-choice, true-false, and short-answer	●	●	●	●	●	●

Literary Response

	K	1	2	3	4	5
listen to stories read aloud	●	●	●	●	●	●
participate actively during a read aloud of predictable and patterned selections	●	●	●	●		
respond through talk, movement, music, art, drama, and writing	●	●	●	●	●	●
describe how illustrations contribute to text	●	●	●	●	●	●
connect, compare, and contrast ideas, themes, and issues across texts	●	●	●	●	●	●
demonstrate understanding of informational texts through writing, illustrating, demonstrations	●	●	●	●	●	●
support interpretations or conclusions with examples from text		●	●	●	●	●
offer observations, make connections, react, speculate, interpret, and raise questions in response to text	●	●	●	●	●	●
interpret texts through journal writing, discussion, enactment, and media	●	●	●	●	●	●
support responses by referring to relevant aspects of the text and own experiences	●	●	●	●	●	●

Inquiry/Research

	K	1	2	3	4	5
identify and form relevant questions for research	●	●	●	●	●	●
use pictures, print, and people to gather and answer questions	●	●	●	●	●	●
draw conclusions from information gathered	●	●	●	●	●	●
locate and use important areas of the library/media center	●	●	●	●	●	●
use alphabetical order to locate information		●	●	●	●	●
recognize and use parts of a book to locate information	●	●	●	●	●	●
use multiple sources to locate information that addresses questions			●	●	●	●
interpret and use graphic sources of information, i.e., charts, graphs, and diagrams	●	●	●	●	●	●
demonstrate learning through productions and displays	●	●	●	●	●	●
organize information in systematic ways		●	●	●	●	●
use compiled information and knowledge to raise additional unanswered questions				●	●	●
use text organizers to locate and organize information				●	●	●
summarize and organize information from multiple sources by taking notes, outlining ideas, or making charts			●	●	●	●

Scope and Sequence

	GRADE	K	1	2	3	4	5
Culture							
connect own experiences with life experiences, language, customs, and cultures of others		●	●	●	●	●	●
compare experiences of characters across cultures		●	●	●	●	●	●
compare text events with own and other readers' experiences		●	●	●	●	●	●
determine distinctive and common characteristics of cultures through wide reading		●	●	●	●	●	●
articulate and discuss themes and connections that cross cultures		●	●	●	●	●	●
LISTENING/SPEAKING							
determine purposes		●	●	●	●	●	●
respond to directions and questions		●	●	●	●	●	●
participate in rhymes, songs, conversations and discussions		●	●	●	●	●	●
listen critically to interpret and evaluate		●	●	●	●	●	●
listen to stories and other texts read aloud		●	●	●	●	●	●
identify musical elements of literary language		●	●	●	●	●	●
connect experiences and ideas with those of others		●	●	●	●	●	●
compare language and oral traditions that reflect customs, regions, and cultures		●	●	●	●	●	●
choose appropriate language for audience, purpose, and occasion		●	●	●	●	●	●
use verbal and nonverbal communication when making announcements, directions, introductions		●	●	●	●	●	●
ask and answer relevant questions, and contribute		●	●	●	●	●	●
present dramatics		●	●	●	●	●	●
gain control of grammar		●	●	●	●	●	●
learn vocabulary of school		●	●	●	●		
use vocabulary to describe ideas, feelings, and experiences		●	●	●	●	●	●
support spoken language using props		●	●	●	●	●	●
retell by summarizing or clarifying		●	●	●	●	●	●
eliminate barriers to effective listening		●	●	●	●	●	●
understand major ideas and supporting evidence		●	●	●	●	●	●
interpret messages, purposes, and perspectives		●	●	●	●	●	●
identify and analyze persuasive techniques				●	●	●	●
distinguish between opinion and fact					●	●	●
monitor own understanding			●	●	●	●	●
listen to proficient models of oral reading		●	●	●	●	●	●
describe how language of literature affects listener		●	●	●	●	●	●
assess language choice and delivery					●	●	●
identify how regional labels/sayings reflect regions and cultures					●	●	●
demonstrate skills that reflect interviewing, reporting, requesting and providing information			●	●	●	●	●

● = direct instruction   ▨ = mastery

	Grade	K	1	2	3	4	5
use effective rate, volume, pitch, tone		●	●	●	●	●	●
give precise directions and instructions in games and tasks		●	●	●	●	●	●
clarify and support with evidence, elaborations and examples			●	●	●	●	●

WRITING

Penmanship/Capitalization/Punctuation

	K	1	2	3	4	5
write own name and other important words	●	●				
write each letter of alphabet, capital and lowercase	●	●				
use phonological knowledge to map sounds to letters, in order to write messages	●	●	●	●	●	●
write messages left to right, top to bottom	●	●	●	●		
gain control of pencil grip, paper position, beginning strokes, posture, letter formation, appropriate size, and spacing	●	●				
use word and letter spacing and margins		●	●			
use capitalization and punctuation, i.e., names, first letters in sentences, periods, question marks, exclamation marks, proper nouns, abbreviations, commas, apostrophes, quotation marks, contractions, possessives	●	●	●	●	●	●
write legibly by selecting cursive or manuscript, as appropriate		●	●	●	●	●

Spelling

	K	1	2	3	4	5
write with proficient spelling of: CVC, CVC silent e, one syllable with blends		●	●	●	●	●
inflectional endings: plurals, verb tenses, drop final e when endings are added			●	●	●	●
single-syllable words with r-controlled vowels, final consonants		●	●	●	●	●
orthographic patterns, i.e., consonant doubling, dropping e, changing y to i			●	●	●	●
use resources to find correct spellings, synonyms, and replacements			●	●	●	●
use conventional spelling of familiar words in final drafts		●	●	●	●	●
spell multisyllabic words using regularly spelled phonogram patterns			●	●	●	●
write with more proficient spelling of contractions, compounds, and homonyms		●	●	●	●	●
open and closed syllables, consonant before -le, and syllable boundary patterns			●	●	●	●
spell words ending in -tion and -sion				●	●	●
spell accurately in final drafts		●	●	●	●	●

Composition/Process

	K	1	2	3	4	5
dictate messages	●	●	●			
write labels, notes, and captions for illustrations, possessions, charts, and centers	●	●	●	●	●	●
write to record ideas and reflections	●	●	●	●	●	●
generate ideas before writing on self-selected topics	●	●	●	●	●	●
generate ideas before writing on assigned topics	●	●	●	●	●	●
develop drafts		●	●	●	●	●
use available technology to compose text	●	●	●	●	●	●
revise selected drafts for varied purposes		●	●	●	●	●
revise drafts for coherence, progression, and logical support of ideas		●	●	●	●	●

Scope and Sequence

	Grade	K	1	2	3	4	5
edit for appropriate grammar, spelling, punctuation, and features of polished writings			●	●	●	●	●
demonstrate understanding of language use and spelling by bringing pieces to final form and "publishing"			●	●	●	●	●
proofread own writing and that of others			●	●	●	●	●
select and use reference materials and resources for writing			●	●	●	●	●
Purposes							
dictate messages		●	●	●	▨	▨	▨
write labels, notes, and captions for illustrations, possessions, charts, and centers		●	●	●	●	●	●
write to record ideas and reflections		●	●	●	●	●	●
write to express, discover, record, develop, reflect, and refine ideas, and to problem solve		●	●	●	●	●	●
write to communicate with a variety of audiences		●	●	●	●	●	●
write in different forms for different purposes		●	●	●	●	●	●
write to influence				●	●	●	●
write to inform		●	●	●	●	●	●
write to entertain		●	●	●	●	●	●
exhibit an identifiable voice in personal narratives and stories				●	●	●	●
choose the appropriate form for own purpose for writing					●	●	●
use literary devices, i.e., suspense, dialogue, figurative language				●	●	●	●
Grammar/Usage/Mechanics							
use nouns and verbs in sentences		●	●	●	●	●	●
compose complete sentences and use appropriate punctuation		●	●	●	●	●	●
use singular and plural forms of regular nouns			●	●	●	●	●
compose sentences with interesting elaborated subjects					●	●	●
edit writing toward standard grammar and usage			●	●	●	●	●
use correct irregular plurals				●	●	●	●
use singular and plural forms of regular nouns, and adjust verbs for agreement			●	●	●	●	●
compose elaborated sentences and use appropriate punctuation					●	●	●
use regular and irregular plurals correctly					●	●	●
write in complete sentences, varying the types				●	●	●	●
employ standard English usage, subject-verb agreement, pronoun referents, and parts of speech			●	●	●	●	●
use adjectives and adverbs			●	●	●	●	●
use prepositional phrases to elaborate written ideas					●	●	●
use conjunctions to connect ideas					●	●	●
use apostrophes in contractions and possessives			●	●	●	●	●
use objective-case pronouns accurately				●	●	●	●

● = direct instruction   ▨ = mastery

	GRADE	K	1	2	3	4	5
Evaluation							
identify the most effective features of a piece by using student and teacher criteria			●	●	●	●	●
respond constructively to others' writing		●	●	●	●	●	●
determine how own writing achieves its purposes			●	●	●	●	●
use published pieces as models		●	●	●	●	●	●
review collection of own work to monitor growth			●	●	●	●	●
apply criteria to evaluate writing			●	●	●	●	●
review a collection of written works to determining its strengths and weaknesses, and to set goals			●	●	●	●	●
Inquiry/Research							
record/dictate questions for investigating		●	●	●	●	●	●
record/dictate own knowledge		●	●	●	●	●	●
take simple notes from sources			●	●	●	●	●
compile notes into outlines, reports, summaries				●	●	●	●
frame questions, to direct research			●	●	●	●	●
organize prior knowledge with graphic organizer		●	●	●	●	●	●
take notes from various sources				●	●	●	●
summarize and organize ideas			●	●	●	●	●
present information in various forms		●	●	●	●	●	●
evaluate own research and raise new questions					●	●	●
Connections							
collaborate with other writers			●	●	●	●	●
correspond with peers or others by e-mail or conventional mail					●	●	●
VIEWING							
Representing/Interpretation							
describe illustrator's choice of style, elements, and media		●	●	●	●	●	●
interpret events and ideas from maps, charts, graphics, video segments, and technology presentations		●	●	●	●	●	●
Representing/Analysis							
interpret and evaluate visual image makers		●	●	●	●	●	●
compare-contrast print, visual, and electronic media		●	●	●	●	●	●
Representing/Production							
select, organize, and produce visuals to complement and extend meanings		●	●	●	●	●	●
produce communications using technology		●	●	●	●	●	●

GRADE K

This index incorporates references to the Teacher's Edition for all six units in Grade K of Literacy Place. For your convenience, the index is divided into three sections, as listed below.

▶ SKILLS AND STRATEGIES

▶ INSTRUCTIONAL ISSUES

▶ LITERATURE

Index

SKILLS AND STRATEGIES

References to the book you're in are in blue. Each unit in Grade K is identified by the initials of its theme.

PV · Personal Voice: Stories About Us

PS · Problem Solving: See It, Solve It

TW · Teamwork: All Together Now!

CE · Creative Expression: Express Yourself

MI · Managing Information: I Spy!

CI · Community Involvement: Join In!

Index

Recognize Literary Genres

CE: T14–T16, T60–T62, T106–T108; **MI:** T14–T16, T60–T62, T106–T108; **CI:** T14–T16, T60–T62, T106–T108

Concept Book, PV: T118–T120; **PS:** T64–T66, T68–T69; **TW:** T18–T20, T22–T23; **MI:** T26–T28, T64–T66, T68–T69, T72–T74; **CI:** T80–T82

Information, PV: T18–T20, T22–T23, T110–T112, T114–T115; **TW:** T110–T112, T127–T128; **MI:** T18–T20, T22–T24, T88–T90, T118–T120; **CI:** T18–T20, T22–T24, T26–T28

Photo Essay, MI: T18–T20, T22–T23, T126–T128

Poetry

Poetry/Song, PV: T14, T18, T26, T30, T34, T35, T46, T50, T62, T64, T72, T76, T80, T92, T96, T110, T118, T122, T134, T138, T142; **PS:** T18, T30, T34, T35, T39, T46, T64, T76, T80, T92, T110, T118, T122, T126, T138, T142; **TW:** T18, T23, T30, T34, T46, T65, T76, T92, T110, T122, T126, T138, T142; **CE:** T18, T28, T30, T46, T50, T76, T80, T92, T122, T138, T142; **MI:** T30, T34, T46, T61, T64, T76, T80, T110, T111, T122, T126, T138, T142; **CI:** T18, T30, T34, T46, T50, T76, T80, T92, T122, T126, T138, T142

Recognize Narrative Forms

Cumulative Story, PS: T80–T82; **TW:** T80–T82; **CE:** T110–T112, T114–T115

Predictable Story, PV: T34–T35, T42–T43, T64–T66, T68–T69; **PS:** T34–T35, T80–T82, T110–T112, T114–T115, T131, T143–T144; **CE:** T18–T20, T22–T23, T34–T36, T110–T112, T114–T115, T88–T90; **MI:** T110–T112, T114–T115, T126–T128; **CI:** T42–T44, T110–T112, T114–T115

Circular Story, PS: T64–T66, T68–T69; **CI:** T42–T44

Vocabulary

Collect Interesting Words, PV: T24; **PS:** T30, T47, T60, T61, T77, T93, T106, T107, T123, T139; **TW:** T14, T15, T31, T47, T60, T61, T62, T77, T93, T128, T136; **CE:** T14, T15, T31, T47, T82, T93, T123, T139; **MI:** T14, T15, T16, T17, T31, T38, T47, T77, T93, T123, T139; **CI:** T31, T47

Facial Expressions/Body Language, PV: T111, T112, T115, T120, T128; **PS:** T74, T75, **TW:** T72, T74; **CE:** T65, T66, T85, T87; **CI:** T74, T117

High-Frequency Words, PV: T24, T31, T40, T47, T70, T77, T86, T93, T116, T123, T132, T139; **PS:** T24, T31, T40, T47, T70, T77, T86, T93, T116, T123, T132, T139; **TW:** T24, T31, T40, T47, T70, T77, T93, T116, T123, T132, T139, T144; **CE:** T24, T31, T40, T47, T70, T77, T86, T93, T116, T123, T130, T132, T139; **MI:** T24, T31, T40, T47, T70, T77, T86, T93, T116, T123, T132, T139; **CI:** T24, T31, T40, T47, T70, T77, T86, T93, T116, T123, T132, T139

Make Word Categories, PV: T46, T70, T86, T114; **PS:** T14, T15, T87, T106, T121; **TW:** T14, T99, T141; **CE:** T41, T52, T111, T117; **MI:** T19, T33, T107; **CI:** T94

Story Vocabulary, PV: T20, T40, T44, T61, T65, T72, T86, T107; **PS:** T42, T61, T108; **TW:** T31, T35, T37, T93, T127, T139; **CE:** T16, T31, T43, T47; **MI:** T47, T61, T77; **CI:** T69

Writing and Language Arts Skills and Strategies

Conventions of Language

Mechanics

Capitalize First Word of Sentence, PV: T74; **PS:** T23, T123, T132; **TW:** T23, T40, T112, T132; **CE:** T132; **MI:** T28, T62, T69; **CI:** T16, T22, T23, T98, T122, T144

Punctuation

Exclamation Mark, PV: T66, T74; **TW:** T122; **CE:** T28, T122; **MI:** T69, T86; **CI:** T30

Period, PV: T74; **PS:** T23, T69; **TW:** T122; **CE:** T120, T132; **MI:** T66, T69, T132; **CI:** T16, T40, T86, T98, T122, T131, T132, T144

Question Mark, PV: T74; **PS:** T20, T23, T69, T123; **TW:** T86, T122, T131; **CE:** T86; **MI:** T66, T69, T132; **CI:** T31, T40, T76, T86, T98, T122, T131, T132, T144

Listening

Demonstrate Active Listening Skills

Follow Directions, PV: T22, T38, T46, T109, T121, T137; **PS:** T50, T90; **TW:** T63, T85, T87, T93, T113, T121, T127, T145; **CE:** T125; **MI:** T39, T41, T64, T79, T99

Listen to a Story/Poem, PV: T14, T15, T18, T19, T26–T27, T30, T34, T35, T42–T43, T46, T50, T62, T64, T67, T72–T73, T76, T80, T81, T85, T88–T89, T92, T96, T110, T118–T119, T134–T135, T138, T142; **PS:** T18, T26–T27, T30, T34, T35, T39, T42–T43, T46, T52, T64, T72–T73, T76, T80, T88–T89, T92, T110, T118–T119, T122, T126, T134–T135, T138, T142; **TW:** T26–T27, T42–T43, T64, T72–T73, T80, T88–T89, T96, T110, T118–T119, T131, T134–T135, T138; **CE:** T26–T27, T30, T34, T42–T43, T46, T50, T72–T73, T88–T89, T118–T119, T126, T134–T135; **MI:** T26–T27, T34, T42–T43, T46, T64, T72–T73, T76, T88–T89, T96, T118–T119, T134–T135, T138, T142; **CI:** T18, T26–T27, T34, T42–T43, T50, T72–T73, T76, T80, T88–T89, T92, T118–T119, T122, T126, T134–T135, T142

Listen to Each Other, to Others, and the Teacher

PV: T14, T15, T18, T19, T22, T23, T24, T26, T27, T30, T31, T34, T35, T38, T42, T43, T46, T47, T60, T61, T64, T65, T68, T69, T70, T72, T73, T74, T76, T77, T80, T81, T86, T88, T89, T92, T96, T106, T107, T110, T111, T114, T118, T119, T126, T127, T134, T135

PS: T14, T15, T18, T19, T22, T23, T24, T26, T27, T30, T31, T34, T35, T42, T43, T46, T47, T60, T61, T64, T65, T68, T69, T72, T73, T74, T76, T77, T80, T81, T86, T88, T89, T92, T106, T107, T110, T111, T114, T118, T119, T126, T127, T134, T135

TW: T14, T15, T18, T19, T22, T23, T24, T26, T27, T30, T31, T34, T35, T42, T43, T46, T47, T60, T61, T64, T65, T68, T69, T72, T73, T74, T76, T77, T80, T81, T86, T88, T89, T92, T106, T107, T110, T111, T114, T118, T119, T126, T127, T134, T135

CE: T14, T15, T18, T19, T22, T23, T24, T26, T27, T30, T31, T34, T35, T42, T43, T46, T47, T60, T61, T64, T65, T68, T69, T72, T73, T74, T76, T77, T80, T81, T86, T88, T89, T92, T106, T107, T110, T111, T114, T118, T119, T126, T127, T134, T135

Index

MI: T14, T15, T18, T19, T22, T23, T24, T26, T27, T30, T31, T34, T35, T42, T43, T46, T47, T60, T61, T64, T65, T68, T69, T72, T73, T74, T76, T77, T80, T81, T86, T88, T89, T92, T106, T107, T110, T111, T114, T118, T119, T126, T127, T134, T135

CI: T14, T15, T18, T19, T22, T23, T24, T26, T27, T30, T31, T34, T35, T42, T43, T46, T47, T60, T61, T64, T65, T68, T69, T72, T73, T74, T76, T77, T80, T81, T86, T88, T89, T92, T106, T107, T110, T111, T114, T118, T119, T126, T127, T134, T135

Listen to Stories on Tape, PV: T18, T36, T64, T68, T76, T79, T110; **PS:** T18, T20, T22, T25, T30, T52, T64, T68, T99, T112, T114; **TW:** T18, T20, T22, T30, T37, T46, T64, T66, T68, T75, T76, T80, T92, T126, T138; **CE:** T18, T20, T22, T23, T34, T53, T88, T90, T92, T110, T112, T114, T115, T122, T125; **MI:** T18, T20, T22, T30, T45, T46, T64, T68, T76, T92, T126, T138; **CI:** T18, T20, T30, T34, T42, T46, T64, T68, T110, T114, T122, T138

Purpose for Listening, PV: T81; **PS:** T134; **TW:** T60; **CE:** T14, T26

Respond to Storytelling, PV: T88–T90; **PS:** T126–T128; **TW:** T80–T83; **CE:** T126–T128; **MI:** T34–T36; **CI:** T34–T36

Respond to What Is Heard

PV: T15, T19, T27, T35, T43, T61, T65, T73, T81, T89, T107, T111, T119, T127, T135

PS: T15, T19, T27, T35, T43, T61, T65, T73, T81, T89, T107, T111, T119, T127, T135

TW: T15, T19, T27, T35, T43, T61, T65, T73, T81, T89, T107, T111, T119, T127, T135

CE: T15, T19, T27, T35, T43, T61, T65, T73, T81, T89, T107, T111, T119, T127, T135

MI: T15, T19, T27, T35, T43, T61, T65, T73, T81, T89, T107, T111, T119, T127, T135

CI: T15, T19, T27, T35, T43, T61, T65, T73, T81, T89, T107, T111, T119, T127, T135

Oral Language

PV: T14, T18, T26, T34, T38, T42, T50, T68, T72, T81, T84, T86, T88, T96, T106, T110, T114, T118, T126, T130, T132, T134, T142

PS: T14, T18, T26, T34, T40, T42, T50, T60, T64, T72, T80, T86, T88, T96, T106, T110, T118, T127, T132, T134, T142

TW: T14, T18, T26, T34, T40, T42, T50, T60, T64, T72, T81, T86, T88, T96, T106, T110, T118, T119, T126, T132, T134, T142

CE: T14, T18, T26, T34, T40, T42, T50, T60, T64, T72, T80, T86, T88, T96, T106, T110, T118, T127, T132, T134, T142

MI: T14, T18, T26, T35, T40, T42, T50, T60, T64, T72, T80, T88, T96, T106, T110, T118, T126, T132, T134, T135, T142

CI: T14, T18, T26, T35, T40, T42, T50, T60, T64, T73, T80, T84, T86, T89, T96, T106, T110, T119, T126, T132, T135, T142

Print Awareness

Add Labels to Drawings to Express Meaning, PV: T29, T41, T45, T47, T60, T69, T97, T123, T142, T143, T144; **PS:** T28, T35, T39, T43, T47, T63, T66, T82, T83, T87, T112, T113, T117, T120, T141, T144; **TW:** T16, T28, T39, T47, T82, T113; **CE:** T17, T21, T25, T28, T35, T44, T60, T62, T66, T67, T81, T91, T108, T116, T120, T128, T133, T144; **MI:** T17, T44, T83, T85, T128; **CI:** T33, T39, T49, T52, T63, T66, T68, T71, T83, T90, T108, T109, T117, T145

Scribble as a Form of Written Communication, PV: T16, T20, T24, T28, T36, T39, T44, T62, T66, T70, T74, T82, T85, T90, T108, T112, T116, T120, T128, T131, T136; **PS:** T16, T20, T24, T28, T36, T39, T44, T62, T66, T70, T74, T82, T85, T90, T108, T112, T116, T120, T128, T131, T136; **TW:** T16, T20, T24, T28, T36, T39, T44, T62, T66, T70, T74, T82, T85, T90, T108, T112, T116, T120, T128, T131, T136; **CE:** T16, T20, T24, T28, T36, T39, T44, T62, T66, T70, T74, T82, T85, T90, T108, T112, T116, T120, T128, T131, T136; **MI:** T16, T20, T24, T28, T36, T39, T44, T62, T66, T70, T74, T82, T85, T90, T108, T112, T116, T120, T128, T131, T136; **CI:** T16, T20, T24, T28, T36, T39, T44, T62, T66, T70, T74, T82, T85, T90, T108, T112, T116, T120, T128, T131, T136

Syntactic Awareness, PV: T16, T18, T19, T20, T24, T44, T70, T90, T116, T119, T128; **PS:** T20, T23, T24, T31, T36, T40, T47, T69, T70, T77, T86, T90, T93, T112, T116, T123, T132, T139; **TW:** T16, T23, T24, T31, T70, T74, T92, T93, T112, T115; **CE:** T14, T28, T31, T33, T46, T47, T90, T108, T116, T120, T123, T136, T139; **MI:** T20, T36, T39, T44, T82, T85, T131, T136; **CI:** T24, T28, T31, T33, T47, T70, T74, T84, T85, T90, T108, T112, T116, T120, T130, T131

Use Drawing to Express Meaning, PV: T16, T17, T20, T25, T28, T29, T32, T36, T38, T39, T44, T47, T62, T66, T70, T74, T82, T83, T85, T86, T90, T93, T94, T108, T110, T115, T120, T125; **PS:** T15, T16, T18, T20, T25, T33, T37, T38, T41, T43, T48, T51, T62, T63, T65, T66, T71, T74, T81, T82, T86, T87, T90, T99, T112, T117, T119, T120, T131, T132, T137; **TW:** T17, T20, T25, T28, T37, T40, T44, T53, T66, T67, T69, T75, T81, T83, T86, T90, T94, T108, T113, T115, T117, T120, T128, T131, T132, T136, T137, T140; **CE:** T19, T28, T36, T37, T40, T41, T44, T67, T69, T74, T81, T82, T83, T85, T90, T91, T106, T108, T111, T112, T116, T120, T121, T124, T127, T128, T132, T133, T136; **MI:** T17, T19, T20, T23, T25, T28, T29, T31, T37, T40, T44, T53, T62, T66, T73, T74, T78, T80, T82, T83, T86, T87, T90, T91, T94, T99, T108, T111, T112, T120, T121, T122, T128, T129, T132, T133; **CI:** T15, T20, T21, T25, T28, T29, T39, T40, T41, T45, T52, T53, T63, T66, T67, T68, T70, T71, T74, T78, T82, T83, T86, T87, T90, T91, T108, T112, T115, T116, T117, T120, T133, T136

Use Upper- and Lower-Case Letters, PS: T30, T47, T60, T61, T77, T93, T106, T107, T123, T139; **TW:** T14, T15, T31, T47, T60, T61, T62, T77, T93, T128, T136; **CE:** T14, T15, T31, T47, T82, T93, T123, T139; **MI:** T14, T15, T16, T17, T31, T38, T47, T77, T93, T123, T139; **CI:** T31, T47

Write From Left to Right, From Top to Bottom, PV: T16, T20, T24, T28, T36, T39, T44, T62, T66, T70, T74, T82, T85, T90, T108, T112, T116, T120, T128, T131, T136; **PS:** T16, T20, T24, T28, T36, T39, T44, T62, T66, T70, T74, T82, T85, T90, T108, T112, T116, T120, T128, T131, T136; **TW:** T16, T20, T24, T28, T36, T39, T44, T62, T66, T70, T74, T82, T85, T90, T108, T112, T116, T120, T128, T131, T136; **CE:** T16, T20, T24, T28, T36, T39, T44, T62, T66, T70, T74, T82, T85, T90, T108, T112, T116, T120, T128, T131, T136; **MI:** T16, T20, T24, T28, T36, T39, T44, T62, T66, T70, T74, T82, T85, T90, T108, T112, T116, T120, T128, T131, T136; **CI:** T16, T20, T24, T28, T36, T39, T44, T62, T66, T70, T74, T82, T85, T90, T108, T112, T116, T120, T128, T131, T136

Write With Spaces Between Units to Represent Words, PV: T16, T20, T24, T28, T36, T39, T44, T62, T66, T70, T74, T82, T85, T90, T108, T112, T116, T120, T128, T131, T136; **PS:** T16, T20, T24, T28, T36, T39, T44, T62, T66, T70, T74, T82, T85, T90, T108, T112, T116, T120, T128, T131, T136; **TW:** T16, T20, T24, T28, T36, T39, T44, T62, T66, T70, T74, T82, T85, T90, T108, T112, T116, T120, T128, T131, T136; **CE:** T16, T20, T24, T28, T36, T39, T44, T62, T66, T70, T74, T82, T85, T90, T108, T112, T116, T120, T128, T131, T136; **MI:** T16, T20, T24, T28, T36, T39, T44, T62, T66, T70, T74, T82, T85, T90, T108, T112, T116, T120, T128, T131, T136; **CI:** T16, T20, T24, T28, T36, T39,

T44, T62, T66, T70, T74, T82, T85, T90, T108, T112, T116, T120, T128, T131, T136

Write With Symbols That Resemble Letters and Letter Shapes, PS: T30, T47, T60, T61, T77, T93, T106, T107, T123, T139; **TW:** T14, T15, T31, T47, T60, T61, T62, T77, T93, T128, T136; **CE:** T14, T15, T31, T47, T82, T93, T123, T139; **MI:** T14, T15, T16, T17, T31, T38, T47, T77, T93, T123, T139; **CI:** T31, T47

Speaking

Demonstrate Speaking Skills
Do a Commercial, TW: T62

Engage in Conversation by Sharing Ideas

PV: T14, T15, T18, T19, T22, T23, T24, T26, T27, T30, T31, T34, T35, T39, T41, T42, T43, T46, T47, T49, T50, T53, T60, T61, T64, T65, T68, T69, T72, T73, T74, T76, T77, T80, T81, T85, T86, T88, T89, T92, T96, T106, T107, T110, T111, T114, T118, T119, T126, T127, T134, T135
PS: T14, T15, T18, T19, T22, T23, T24, T26, T27, T30, T31, T34, T35, T42, T43, T46, T47, T52, T60, T61, T62, T64, T65, T66, T68, T70, T72, T73, T75, T77, T78, T80, T81, T86, T88, T89, T92, T106, T107, T110, T111, T114, T118, T119, T126, T127, T134, T135

TW: T14, T15, T18, T19, T22, T23, T24, T26, T27, T30, T31, T34, T35, T42, T43, T46, T47, T60, T61, T64, T65, T68, T69, T72, T73, T74, T76, T77, T80, T81, T86, T88, T89, T92, T106, T107, T110, T111, T114, T118, T119, T126, T127, T134, T135

CE: T14, T15, T18, T19, T22, T23, T24, T26, T27, T30, T31, T34, T35, T42, T43, T46, T47, T60, T61, T64, T65, T68, T69, T72, T73, T74, T76, T77, T80, T81, T86, T88, T89, T92, T106, T107, T110, T111, T114, T118, T119, T126, T127, T134, T135

MI: T14, T15, T18, T19, T22, T23, T24, T26, T27, T30, T31, T34, T35, T42, T43, T46, T47, T60, T61, T64, T65, T68, T69, T72, T73, T74, T76, T77, T80, T81, T86, T88, T89, T92, T106, T107, T110, T111, T114, T118, T119, T126, T127, T134, T135

CI: T14, T15, T18, T19, T22, T23, T24, T26, T27, T30, T31, T34, T35, T42, T43, T46, T47, T60, T61, T64, T65, T68, T69, T72, T73, T74, T76, T77, T80, T81, T86, T88, T89, T92, T106, T107, T110, T111, T114, T118, T119, T126, T127, T134, T135

Give Directions, PV: T38, T91; **TW:** T87, T99, T117

Orally Present Poetry, PV: T26, T34, T35, T36, T37, T46, T67, T72, T118; **PS:** T73, T76, T92, T112, T125, T126, T139; **TW:** T14, T31, T60, T136, T139; **CE:** T14, T31, T35, T36, T37; **MI:** T31, T47, T60, T106

Participate in Choral Reading, PV: T36, T62; **PS:** T69, T115; **TW:** T16, T35, T44; **CE:** T23, T26, T36, T62, T112; **MI:** T74, T128; **CI:** T115, T128

Participate in Echo Reading, PV: T35; **TW:** T115; **CE:** T19, T20, T35, T44, T64, T111; **MI:** T117; **CI:** T19, T81

Recite a Chant, PV: T26, T34, T35, T36, T37, T46, T67, T72, T118; **PS:** T73, T112, T132, T139; **TW:** T14, T31, T60, T123, T136, T139; **CE:** T14, T31, T35, T36, T37, T47, T95, T123; **MI:** T31, T47, T60, T106; **CI:** T31, T123

Role Play, PV: T20, T21, T41, T71, T82, T87; **PS:** T79; **TW:** T33, T35, T37, T74, T120, T129; **CE:** T29, T44, T82, T87, T136, T137; **MI:** T40; **CI:** T26, T63, T70, T108, T120, T137

Share Experiences

PV: T14, T15, T18, T19, T27, T39, T40, T64, T65, T71, T81, T83, T84, T89,

T91, T111, T118, T127
PS: T35, T43, T61, T65, T73, T81, T89, T111, T118, T119, T127, T135
TW: T15, T19, T27, T35, T43, T61, T65, T73, T81, T89, T127, T135
CE: T15, T18, T19, T20, T24, T25, T26, T27, T29, T32, T34, T35, T39, T40, T43, T58
MI: T15, T19, T27, T35, T42, T61, T65, T73, T127, T131, T135
CI: T15, T19, T27, T35, T36, T43, T61, T65, T73, T81, T89, T107, T111, T119, T127, T131, T135

Sing a Song, PV: T14, T30, T34, T50, T76, T79, T110; **PS:** T34, T39, T46, T64, T76, T110, T142; **TW:** T18, T34, T39, T50, T64, T80, T96, T106, T110, T126, T142; **CE:** T18, T26, T28, T34, T47, T51, T64, T80, T85, T92, T95, T96, T106, T108, T110, T126; **MI:** T18, T26, T30, T34, T64, T76, T110, T126; **CI:** T18, T34, T38, T53, T84, T85, T93, T96, T99, T111, T122, T127, T128, T145

Speak in Complete Sentences, PV: T14, T15, T18, T20, T22, T34, T35, T37, T38, T39, T42, T43, T44, T47, T49, T51, T64, T66, T67, T68, T69, T70, T71, T75, T77, T81, T86, T88, T89, T92, T106, T107, T110, T111, T114, T118, T119, T126, T127, T134, T135; **PS:** T14, T15, T18, T19, T22, T23, T24, T26, T27, T30, T31, T34, T35, T42, T43, T46, T47, T60, T61, T64, T65, T68, T69, T72, T73, T74, T76, T77, T80, T81, T86, T88, T89, T92, T106, T107, T110, T111, T114, T118, T119, T126, T127, T134, T135; **TW:** T14, T15, T18, T19, T22, T23, T24, T26, T27, T30, T31, T34, T35, T42, T43, T46, T47, T60, T61, T64, T65, T68, T69, T72, T73, T74, T76, T77, T80, T81, T86, T88, T89, T92, T106, T107, T110, T111, T114, T118, T119, T126, T127, T134, T135; **CE:** T14, T15, T18, T19, T22, T23, T24, T26, T27, T30, T31, T34, T35, T42, T43, T46, T47, T60, T61, T64, T65, T68, T69, T72, T73, T74, T76, T77, T80, T81, T86, T88, T89, T92, T106, T107, T110, T111, T114, T118, T119, T126, T127, T134, T135; **MI:** T14, T15, T18, T19, T22, T23, T24, T26, T27, T30, T31, T34, T35, T42, T43, T46, T47, T60, T61, T64, T65, T68, T69, T72, T73, T74, T76, T77, T80, T81, T86, T88, T89, T92, T106, T107, T110, T111, T114, T118, T119, T126, T127, T134, T135; **CI:** T14, T15, T18, T19, T22, T23, T24, T26, T27, T30, T31, T34, T35, T42, T43, T46, T47, T60, T61, T64, T65, T68, T69, T72, T73, T74, T76, T77, T80, T81, T86, T88, T89, T92, T106, T107, T110, T111, T114, T118, T119, T126, T127, T134, T135

Speak to Take a Telephone Message, PV: T49

Tell/Retell a Story, PV: T28, T37, T67, T69, T82, T83, T85, T90, T97, T131; **PS:** T20, T51, T52, T62, T65, T74, T82, T99, T119, T120, T128; **TW:** T16, T28, T44, T82; **CE:** T28, T36, T39, T73, T74, T75, T81, T82, T89, T108, T120, T128; **MI:** T28, T36, T51, T120; **CI:** T28, T37, T44, T66, T97, T135

Tell Jokes and Riddles, PS: T18, T20, T36, T79; **TW:** T61; **MI:** T25, T67

Understand Concepts of Print

Directionality (see Track Print From Left to Right)
Identify Punctuation Marks (Period, Question Mark, Exclamation Mark), PV: T61, T66, T74; **PS:** T20, T23, T69, T112, T123, T131; **TW:** T86, T122, T131; **CE:** T16, T28, T86, T120, T122, T132; **MI:** T66, T69, T86, T122, T132; **CI:** T16, T30, T31, T76, T86, T122, T131, T132, T144
Recognize Letter, Word, Sentence Boundaries, PV: T14, T23, T30, T40, T44, T46, T69, T76, T77, T92, T94, T111, T115, T124, T140; **PS:** T23, T69, T69, T76, T86, T92, T115, T132, T138; **TW:** T23, T30, T40, T46, T69, T76, T86, T92, T132, T138; **CE:** T23, T30, T40, T46, T69, T76, T122, T132, T138; **MI:** T20, T23, T30, T40, T46, T69, T76, T82, T92, T122, T132, T138; **CI:** T20, T23, T30, T40, T46, T69, T76, T82, T86, T92, T115, T122, T132, T138

T131, T136; **MI:** T16, T20, T24, T28, T36, T39, T44, T62, T66, T70, T74, T82, T85, T90, T108, T112, T116, T120, T128, T131, T136; **CI:** T16, T20, T24, T28, T36, T39, T44, T62, T66, T70, T74, T82, T85, T90, T108, T112, T116, T120, T128, T131, T136

Write a Story Innovation, PV: T82, T121; **PS:** T70, T82, T116; **TW:** T28, T70, T74; **CE:** T20, T24, T82, T108, T112, T120, T131; **MI:** T82, T128; **CI:** T16, T66, T128

Write About Information Books, TW: T62; **MI:** T16, T20, T24, T36, T37, T39, T44, T51, T66, T70, T85, T90, T108, T112, T116, T120, T128; **CI:** T20, T24, T39, T82, T90, T108, T116, T131, T136

Write Compound Words, TW: T66

Write Descriptive Words, PV: T20, T39, T90; **PS:** T28, T29, T39, T42, T74, T80, T123; **TW:** T36, T106; **CI:** T44

Write Name, PV: T41, T49, T61, T77, T79, T91, T95, T117

Write Rhyming Sentences/Phrases, PV: T36, T62, T109; **TW:** T90, T133; **CI:** T120

Write Sentences, PV: T120; **PS:** T24, T36, T62, T83, T90, T93; T16, T20, T24, T28, T36, T39, T44, T62, T66, T70, T74, T82, T85, T90, T108, T112, T116, T120, T128, T131, T136; **TW:** T24, T70, T108, T112, T116, T120, T131; **CE:** T16, T24, T74, T90, T116, T136; **MI:** T28, T79, T131, T136; **CI:** T24, T27, T68, T70, T84, T108, T112, T114, T116, T130, T131

Write Verses to a Familiar Song, PV: T36; **CE:** T85; **CI:** T85

Integrated Curriculum Activities

Center Workshops

Alphabet, PV: T17, T33, T63, T79, T95; **PS:** T17, T33, T45, T49, T63, T95, T109, T125, T141; **TW:** T33, T49, T79, T91; **CE:** T63, T79, T125; **MI:** T49, T79, T125; **CI:** T33

Art, PV: T33, T41, T67, T75, T83, T87, T91, T109, T117, T121, T125; **PS:** T17, T21, T25, T29, T37, T41, T49, T63, T67, T71, T75, T83, T87, T109, T113, T117, T121, T129, T141; **TW:** T17, T29, T41, T63, T71, T83, T91, T109, T113, T121, T125, T129, T141; **CE:** T17, T21, T33, T37, T45, T60, T75, T83, T91, T117, T121, T129, T133, T137; **MI:** T17, T21, T29, T37, T41, T63, T67, T83, T91, T113, T117, T129, T133, T141; **CI:** T21, T29, T45, T63, T71, T75, T91, T109, T113, T121

Blocks, PV: T141; **PS:** T41; **TW:** T75; **CI:** T17, T41, T83, T133

Cooking, PV: T109, T121, T137; **PS:** T79; **TW:** T37, T45, T63, T71, T87, T113, T117, T121, T125; **CE:** T45, T95; **MI:** T137

Dramatic Play, PV: T21, T41, T49, T71, T87, T113, T137, T141; **PS:** T75, T79, T125, T129; **TW:** T37, T79, T133; **CE:** T17, T29, T41, T137; **MI:** T67, T91; **CI:** T17, T71, T75, T109, T117, T137

Games, PV: T25, T29, T45, T63, T91, T125; **PS:** T33, T71, T103, T113, T137; **TW:** T45, T95; **CE:** T41, T75, T109, T121, T133; **MI:** T41, T95; **CI:** T49, T79, T95

Health & Fitness, PV: T37; **TW:** T33, T49; **CE:** T125; **MI:** T109; **CI:** T113

Listening, PV: T25, T67, T79, T133; **PS:** T25; **CE:** T33, T113; **MI:** T79; **CI:** T79

Math, PV: T17, T71, T75, T83, T95, T113; **PS:** T21, T29, T87, T121, T137; **TW:** T17, T21, T25, T83, T95, T109, T129, T141; **CE:** T49, T67, T83, T117, T141; **MI:** T45, T75, T87, T125; **CI:** T29, T67, T95, T117, T121

Music & Movement. PS: T95; **TW:** T67, T75; **CE:** T25, T29, T79, T87, T95; **MI:** T33, T63, T71, T129; **CI:** T129

Ongoing Project, CI: T17, T21

Science, PV: T37, T129; **PS:** T37, T45, T67, T91, T117, T133; **TW:** T29, T137; **CE:** T21, T25, T37, T49, T67, T71, T91, T113, T141; **MI:** T21, T25, T29, T33, T45, T83, T113, T117, T121, T133, T137, T141; **CI:** T21, T25, T45, T67, T87, T129

Social Studies, PV: T21, T129; **TW:** T25, T41, T67, T87; **CE:** T87; **MI:** T71; **CI:** T63, T83, T91, T133, T137

Writing, PV: T29, T45, T49, T117, T121, T133; **PS:** T83, T133; **TW:** T41, T117, T133; **CE:** T109; **MI:** T25, T49, T87, T95, T109; **CI:** T25, T33, T41, T49, T87, T125, T141

Connections

Science, PV: T82
Social Studies, CI: T62

Everyday Literacies

Research and Study Skills

Follow Directions (see Follow Directions under Demonstrate Active Listening Skills)

Graphs, PV: T75, T95, T113; **TW:** T21, T25, T95; **CE:** T66; **CI:** T29

Maps, PS: T71, T85, T87, T134; **MI:** T17; **CI:** T85, T131

Use Parts of a Book, PV: T16, T23, T62, T78, T79, T115, T125; **CI:** T69

Use Reference Sources, PV: T29, T45, T71, T85, T107, T133; **PS:** T14, T33, T37, T45, T63, T99; **TW:** T18, T87, T109; **CI:** T21, T29, T63, T71, T87, T88, T109, T118

Kindergarten Concepts (ALSO SEE Acquiring World Knowledge)

Colors, PS: T23, T25, T32, T39, T41, T49, T66, T86, T94, T121, T124, T131, T133, T137; **TW:** T14, T17, T32, T48, T61, T64, T78, T81, T94, T109, T116, T132, T140, T141; **CE:** T47; **MI:** T67; **CI:** T118

Days, Months, Year on Calendar, PV: T72, T73, T75; **TW:** T18–T20; **CI:** T29, T89

Numbers, PS: T120, T132; **TW:** T129, T132; **CE:** T49; **MI:** T73, T74, T75

Opposites, PV: T43, T45, T65; **PS:** T26, T28, T43; **TW:** T36; **CI:** T64

Positional Relationships, PV: T16, T22, T34, T38, T60, T65, T92; **PS:** T115; **TW:** T35; **CE:** T79; **CI:** T43

Shapes, PS: T18, T21, T23, T137; **TW:** T17, T45, T71, T75, T81, T109, T141; **CE:** T15, T33, T45, T47, T106; **MI:** T21, T26, T29, T65, T67, T75, T141; **CI:** T75

Transportation, PV: T69, T71; **PS:** T85; **CI:** T14, T15, T60, T63, T106, T132

Index

INSTRUCTIONAL ISSUES

*Index

Journal Opportunities

PV	T16, T20, T23, T28, T32, T36, T40, T44, T48, T62, T66, T69, T74, T78, T86, T90, T94, T108, T112, T120, T124, T128, T132, T136, T140
PS:	T16, T20, T23, T28, T32, T36, T40, T44, T48, T62, T66, T69, T74, T78, T82, T86, T90, T94, T108, T112, T116, T120, T124, T128, T132, T136, T140
TW:	T16, T20, T23, T28, T32, T36, T40, T44, T48, T62, T66, T69, T74, T78, T86, T90, T94, T108, T115, T120, T124, T128, T132, T136, T140
CE:	T16, T20, T23, T28, T32, T36, T40, T44, T48, T62, T66, T69, T74, T78, T82, T86, T90, T94, T108, T112, T115, T120, T124, T128, T132, T136, T140
MI:	T16, T20, T23, T28, T32, T36, T40, T44, T48, T62, T66, T69, T74, T78, T86, T90, T94, T108, T112, T116, T120, T124, T128, T132, T136, T140
CI:	T16, T20, T23, T28, T32, T36, T40, T44, T48, T62, T66, T69, T74, T78, T86, T90, T94, T108, T112, T116, T120, T124, T128, T132, T136, T140

Mentors

Chapin, Tom, **CI:** T6, T11, T57, T103
Mora, Pat, **CE:** T6, T11, T57, T103
Powell, Steve, **MI:** T6, T11, T57, T103
Twumasi, Kwaku, **TW:** T6, T11, T57, T103
Wada, Honey, **PV:** T6, T11, T57, T103
Wible, Becky, **PS:** T6, T11, T57, T103

Places

Gardening Center, **MI:** T99
Performance Stage, **CI:** T99
Restaurant, **TW:** T99
Storytelling Corner, **PV:** T99

Projects

"All About You and Me in School," **PV:** T145
"Animals Say Hello" Big Book, **CE:** T43
Big Book of Family Members, **PV:** T99
Big Book of Menus, **TW:** T145
Big Book of Recipes, **TW:** T99

Index

Modify Instruction

LITERATURE

Genre

ABC Books

Concept Books

Emergent Readers

My Books

High-Frequency Reader

WiggleWorks Books

Fantasy

Fiction

TEACHER'S EDITION

Acknowledgments

Grateful acknowledgment is made to the following sources for permission to reprint from previously published material. The publisher has made diligent efforts to trace the ownership of all copyrighted material in this volume and believes that all necessary permissions have been secured. If any errors or omissions have inadvertently been made, proper corrections will gladly be made in future editions.

Cover: Cynthia Jabar for Scholastic Inc.

"One Elephant" from CIRCLE TIME ACTIVITIES FOR YOUNG CHILDREN by Deya Brashears and Sharron Werlin Krull. Copyright © 1981 by Deya Brashears and Sharron Werlin Krull. Produced by DMC Publications (Ft. Collins, CO), distributed by Gryphon House, Inc. (Mt. Rainier, MD).

"The Three Billy Goats Gruff" as told by Margaret H. Lippert from ONCE UPON A TIME CHILDREN'S ANTHOLOGY, senior authors: Virginia A. Arnold and Carl B. Smith. Copyright © 1988 by Macmillan Publishing Company. Published by Macmillan/McGraw-Hill School Division of McGraw-Hill School Publishing Company.

Sentence Strips: Text for sentence strips adapted from IS YOUR MAMA A LLAMA? by Deborah Guarino. Text copyright © 1989 by Deborah Guarino. Published by Scholastic Inc. All rights reserved.

Book Credits: Cover from ANANSI THE SPIDER: A TALE FROM THE ASHANTI adapted and illustrated by Gerald McDermott. Copyright © 1972 by Landmark Production, Inc. Published by Scholastic Inc., by arrangement with Henry Holt and Company. Cover and spot art from APPLES AND ALLIGATORS AND ALSO ALPHABETS by Odette and Bruce Johnson. Copyright © 1990 by Odette and Bruce Johnson. Published by Scholastic Inc., by arrangement with Oxford University Press. Cover from BIRDS ON STAGE by Saturnino Romay, illustrated by Claude Martinot. Copyright © 1994 by Scholastic Inc. Published by Scholastic Inc. Cover from BOOTS by Anne Schreiber and Arbo Doughty, illustrated by Robin Ballard. Copyright © 1994 by Scholastic Inc. Published by Scholastic Inc. Cover and spot art from CAPS FOR SALE by Esphyr Slobodkina. Illustrations copyright © 1940, 1947, and renewed © 1968 by Esphyr Slobodkina. Published by Scholastic Inc., by arrangement with Addison-Wesley Publishing Company, Inc. Cover and spot art from CARLOS AND THE SQUASH PLANT by Jan Romero Stevens, illustrated by Jeanne Arnold. Illustrations copyright © 1993 by Jeanne Arnold. Published by Scholastic Inc., by arrangement with Northland Publishing Company. Cover and spot art from CORDUROY by Don Freeman. Copyright © 1968 by Don Freeman. Published by Scholastic Inc., by arrangement with Puffin Books, a division of Penguin Putnam Inc. Cover and spot art from I WENT WALKING by Sue Williams, illustrated by Julie Vivas. Illustrations copyright © 1989 by Julie Vivas. Published by Scholastic Inc., by arrangement with Harcourt Brace & Co. Cover from IS YOUR MAMA A LLAMA? by Deborah Guarino, illustrated by Steven Kellogg. Illustrations copyright © 1989 by Steven Kellogg. Published by Scholastic Inc. BLUE RIBBON is a registered trademark of Scholastic Inc. Cover from THE THREE BEARS by Paul Galdone. Copyright © 1972 by Paul Galdone. Published by Scholastic Inc., by arrangement with Clarion Books, a Houghton Mifflin Company imprint. Cover from WHAT AM I? by N. N. Charles, illustrated by Leo and Diane Dillon. Illustrations copyright © 1994 by Leo and Diane Dillon. Published by Scholastic Inc., by arrangement with The Blue Sky Press, an imprint of Scholastic Inc. Cover and spot art from WHERE'S MY TEDDY? by Jez Alborough. Illustrations copyright © 1992 by Jez Alborough. Published by Scholastic Inc., by arrangement with Candlewick Press.

Photography and Illustration Credits

Photos: Photo Stylists: Gayna Hoffman, Shawna Johnston. p. T6: Becky Wible for Scholastic Inc. p. T15: Randy Roderiguez for Scholastic Inc. p. T16: Ana Esperanza Nance for Scholastic Inc. p. T17: Ana Esperanza Nance for Scholastic Inc. p. T19: David Mager for Scholastic Inc. p. T21: Ana Esperanza Nance for Scholastic Inc. David Mager for Scholastic Inc. p. T23: David Mager for Scholastic Inc. p. T25: Ana Esperanza Nance for Scholastic Inc. p. T27: Ana Esperanza Nanc for Scholastic Inc. p. T28: Ana Esperanza Nance for Scholastic Inc. p. T29: Ana Esperanza Nance for Scholastic Inc. Randy Rodriguez for Scholastic Inc. p. T32: Ana Esperanza Nance for Scholastic Inc. p. T33: Randy Rodriguez for Scholastic Inc. p. T35: Kevin Schafer for Scholastic Inc. p. T36: Ana Esperanza Nance for Scholastic Inc. p. T37: Ana Esperanza Nance for Scholastic Inc. © Francis Lepine/Animals, Animals. p. T41: Ana Esperanza Nance for Scholastic Inc. Randy Rodriguez for Scholastic Inc. p. T43: Ana Esperanza Nance for Scholastic Inc. p. T44: Ana Esperanza Nance for Scholastic Inc. p. T45: Ana Esperanza Nance for Scholastic Inc. p. T48: David Mager for Scholastic Inc. p. T49: Ana Esperanza Nance for Scholastic Inc. Randy Rodriguez for Scholastic Inc. p. T50: Clara Von Aich for Scholastic Inc. p. T52: Ana Esperanza Nance for Scholastic Inc. p. T53: Randy Rodriguez for Scholastic Inc. p. T63: Ana Esperanza Nance for Scholastic Inc. p. T67: Ana Esperanza Nance for Scholastic Inc. Francis Clark Westfield for Scholastic Inc. p. T70: Clara Von Aich for Scholastic Inc. p. T71: Ana Esperanza Nance for Scholastic Inc. Randy Rodriguez for Scholastic Inc. p. T72: Ana Esperanza Nance for Scholastic Inc. p. T74: Clara Von Aich for Scholastic Inc. p. T75: Ana Esperanza Nance for Scholastic Inc. Randy Rodriguez for Scholastic Inc. p. T78: Randy Rodriguez for Scholastic Inc. p. T79: David Mager for Scholastic Inc. p. T83: Ana Esperanza Nance for Scholastic Inc. p. T87: Ana Esperanza Nance for Scholastic Inc. Randy Rodriguez for Scholastic Inc. p. T89: David Mager for Scholastic Inc. p. T91: Ken O'Donoghue for Scholastic Inc. p. T94: Francis Clark Westfield for Scholastic Inc. p. T95: Ana Esperanza Nance for Scholastic Inc. p. T96: David Mager for Scholastic Inc. p. T99: Clara Von Aich for Scholastic Inc. p. T108: Ana Esperanza Nance for Scholastic Inc. p. T109: Ana Esperanza Nance for Scholastic Inc. Ken O'Donoghue for Scholastic Inc. p. T113: Ana Esperanza Nance for Scholastic Inc. p. T116: © Joan Baron/The Stock Market Inc. © ZEFA Germany/The Stock Market Inc. p. T117: Ana Esperanza Nance for Scholastic Inc. © Renee Lynn/Photo Researchers, Inc. p. T118: © George Godfrey/Animals, Animals. p. T120: Ana Esperanza Nance for

Scholastic Inc. David Mager for Scholastic Inc. p. T121: David Mager for Scholastic Inc. p. T124: Ken O'Donoghue for Scholastic Inc. p. T125: Ana Esperanza Nance for Scholastic Inc. Randy Rodriguez for Scholastic Inc. p. T128: Frank Rossotto for Scholastic Inc. p. T129: Ana Esperanza Nance for Scholastic Inc. David Mager for Scholastic Inc. p. T131: Clara Von Aich for Scholastic Inc. p. T133: Ana Esperanza Nance for Scholastic Inc. Randy Rodriguez for Scholastic Inc. p. T134: © Stephen Dalton/Animals, Animlals. p. T135: Ana Esperanza Nance for Scholastic Inc. p. T136: Ana Esperanza Nance for Scholastic Inc. p. T137: Ana Esperanza Nance for Scholastic Inc. p. T140: Ana Esperanza Nance for Scholastic Inc. p. T141: Ana Esperanza Nance for Scholastic Inc. p. T142: © ZEFA Germany/The Stock Market, Inc. p. T144: Randy Rodriguez for Scholastic Inc. p. T145: Randy Rodriguez for Scholastic Inc. p. T179: Jeanette Gowd for Scholastic Inc. p. T189: John Shefelbine for Scholastic Inc.

Upfront pages: All reduced facsimiles of Student Anthologies, Teacher's Editions, ancillary components, and interior pages are credited, if necessary, in their original publication format.

Illustrations: p. T81: Charlotte Thomas for Scholastic Inc.

a b c d

e f g h

i j k l

m n o p

q r s t

u v w x

y z a e

i o u

small
letters

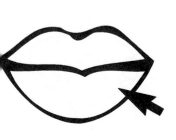   

Teacher Note: The above picture cards are: bat, bee, bus, cat, coat, cup, dog, duck, fan, fish, fox, leaf, lip, log, man, moon.

Copyright © Scholastic Inc.

Teacher Note: The above picture cards are: mop, nest, nose, nut, pan, pen, pig, ring, rock, run, six, sock, sun, ten, tie, top.